AUSTRALIA'S MOST DANGEROUS ANIMALS

By Karen McGhee and Kathy Riley

CONTENTS

SPIDERS

STINGERS, SNAPPERS AND SLASHERS

SHARKS UP CLOSE

A shark is a type of fish. Instead of having a bony skeleton like other fish, its skeleton is made of cartilage. Cartilage is what your ears are made of. Of course, the cartilage in a shark is much thicker than your ears!

CAUDAL FIN

SECOND DORSAL FIN

TAIL

Most sharks move their tail from side to side to swim through the water.

ANAL FIN

PELVIC FIN

FEROCIOUS FACT!

Sharks have up to seven rows of teeth. Every time a shark loses or wears down a tooth, the one behind it moves forward to take its place. Some sharks will lose up to 35,000 teeth in a lifetime. Sharks have differently shaped teeth, depending on what they eat. A shark that eats fish has slender, pointy teeth to help it catch and hold onto its prey. Sharks that eat krill and plankton have very small teeth and hardly use them at all.

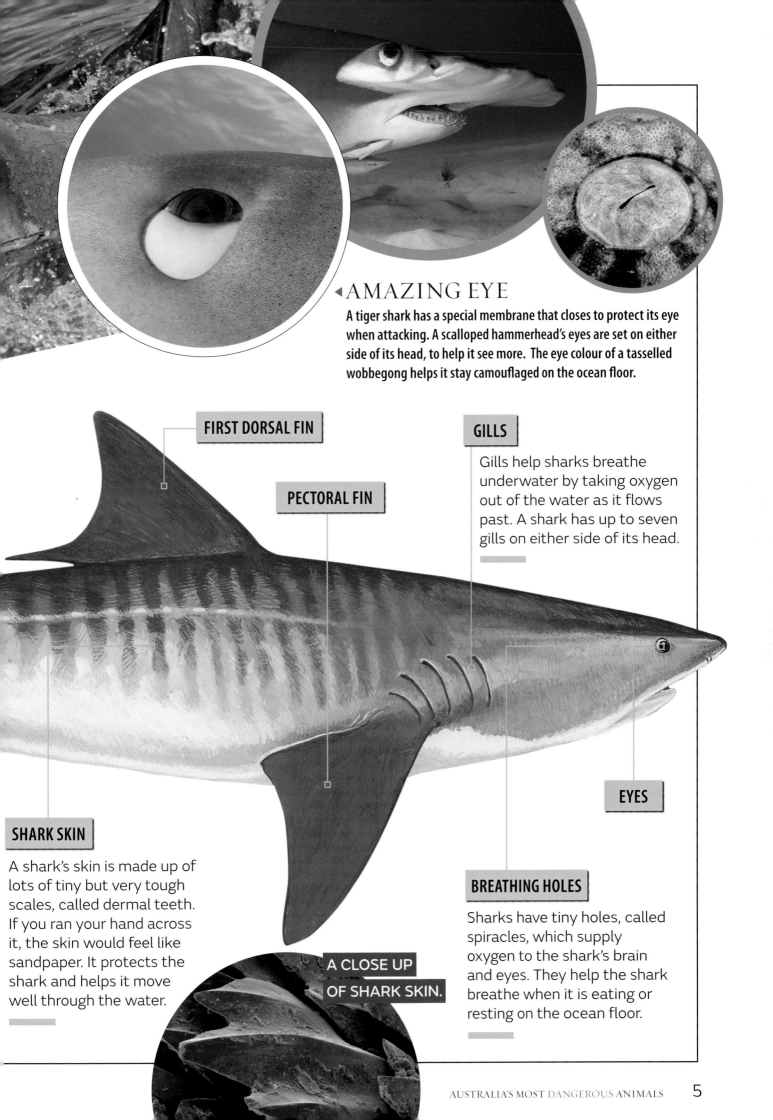

◄AMAZING EYE

A tiger shark has a special membrane that closes to protect its eye when attacking. A scalloped hammerhead's eyes are set on either side of its head, to help it see more. The eye colour of a tasselled wobbegong helps it stay camouflaged on the ocean floor.

FIRST DORSAL FIN

PECTORAL FIN

GILLS

Gills help sharks breathe underwater by taking oxygen out of the water as it flows past. A shark has up to seven gills on either side of its head.

SHARK SKIN

A shark's skin is made up of lots of tiny but very tough scales, called dermal teeth. If you ran your hand across it, the skin would feel like sandpaper. It protects the shark and helps it move well through the water.

EYES

BREATHING HOLES

Sharks have tiny holes, called spiracles, which supply oxygen to the shark's brain and eyes. They help the shark breathe when it is eating or resting on the ocean floor.

A CLOSE UP OF SHARK SKIN.

SHARK SHAPES

There are hundreds of sharks in the world and they come in many different shapes, sizes and colours.

▲ Thresher sharks
UP TO 5.7M

The long, pointy tail of a thresher shark is a mighty weapon. These sharks use it to herd small schooling fishes and then to stun them in order to eat them.

▼ Blacktip reef shark
UP TO 1.4M

This is a common shape among shark species: round in the middle and tapering to a point at each end. This design helps sharks to move through the water using as little energy as possible.

▲ Port Jackson shark
UP TO 1.65M

This shark forages around the sea floor at night for starfishes, sea urchins, sea cucumbers and molluscs. Its blunt head and flat front teeth help it to catch and crush the hard shells of its prey. It also has a spine on each of its dorsal fins.

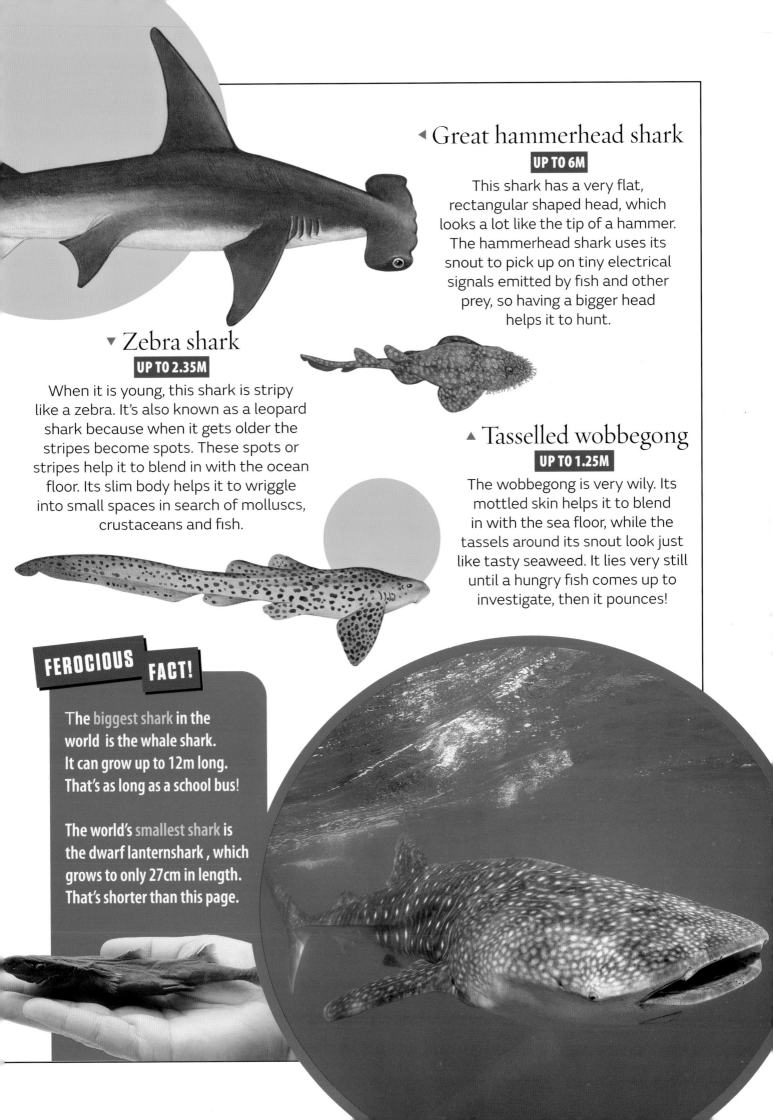

◂ Great hammerhead shark

UP TO 6M

This shark has a very flat, rectangular shaped head, which looks a lot like the tip of a hammer. The hammerhead shark uses its snout to pick up on tiny electrical signals emitted by fish and other prey, so having a bigger head helps it to hunt.

▾ Zebra shark

UP TO 2.35M

When it is young, this shark is stripy like a zebra. It's also known as a leopard shark because when it gets older the stripes become spots. These spots or stripes help it to blend in with the ocean floor. Its slim body helps it to wriggle into small spaces in search of molluscs, crustaceans and fish.

▴ Tasselled wobbegong

UP TO 1.25M

The wobbegong is very wily. Its mottled skin helps it to blend in with the sea floor, while the tassels around its snout look just like tasty seaweed. It lies very still until a hungry fish comes up to investigate, then it pounces!

FEROCIOUS FACT!

The biggest shark in the world is the whale shark. It can grow up to 12m long. That's as long as a school bus!

The world's smallest shark is the dwarf lanternshark, which grows to only 27cm in length. That's shorter than this page.

GREAT WHITE SHARK

DEADLY FACTOR:

9/10

Fact File

OTHER NAMES: White shark, white pointer.

LENGTH: Up to 6m.

DIET: Fish, squid, crustaceans, other sharks, sea turtles, seals, sea lions, dead or rotting animals.

DISTRIBUTION: Around Australia but more commonly found along the southern coast between Exmouth in Western Australia and southern Queensland.

HABITAT: Mainly along coasts, in a wide range of water temperatures.

BREEDING: A female great white shark gives birth to a live pup only once every three years. The newborn pup can be up to 1.5m long.

TRUE OR FALSE?

Female great white sharks are bigger than the males.

A: True

? DID YOU KNOW?

The teeth of a great white are the largest of any living shark. This tooth is actual size!

FEROCIOUS FACT!

A 3m male great white shark known as 'Shark 28' holds the current record for the longest known shark migration. After being tagged in Ballina in northern NSW in 2016, it swam more than 28,000km in 686 days around the Australian coastline from Bundaberg, Queensland, south and west to Margaret River in Western Australia. In the study, some sharks swam up 70km in a day and some non-stop for up to 30 days.

DID YOU KNOW?

The jaws of a great white shark can deliver a bone-crunching bite that is more than 20 times stronger than a human's!

SHARK ALERT!

The number of great white sharks in the ocean has dropped dramatically in the last 50 years. These sharks are now protected in Australian waters which means it is illegal to harm one.

WHERE DO SHARKS LIVE?

Sharks live in oceans all over the world. Some even live in rivers and lakes. Factors affecting where sharks live include water depth, temperature and the availability of both food and mates.

▼ On the move

With so much water everywhere, it's not surprising that sharks travel. Some sharks will cover many thousands of kilometres in search of food or mates. Pelagic sharks, like the great white shark, will roam across entire oceans. Other sharks stay close to land but still migrate long distances. Some sharks like to stay in the same area and not travel too far.

▼ Tag, you're it!

In order to learn more about sharks, including where they travel, researchers will catch a shark and put a special tag on it. Then they let it go. They can then track the movement and behaviour of that shark on a computer.

DID YOU KNOW?
A whitetip reef shark spends 98 per cent of its day resting in the same spot. As soon as the sun sets, it goes hunting for food.

? **DID YOU KNOW?**

Tiger sharks live in warm tropical waters.

GREENLAND SHARKS CAN LIVE UP TO 500 YEARS.

FEROCIOUS FACT!

Water temperature is a big factor in where different sharks choose to live. Many shark species prefer tropical water, where the temperature is always 21°C or higher, which is nice and warm. Tropical sharks include the tiger, whale and bull shark. A few shark species live in water that is less than 5°C, which is close to freezing. These are called polar sharks. The Greenland and dogfish shark are examples of polar sharks. Some sharks, like the great white shark, like to stay in water that is not too warm or too cold. This is called temperate water.

20° — **Tropical**

15° — **Temperate**

10°

5° — **Polar**

SHALLOW OR DEEP

Sharks that live deep in the ocean are called pelagic. The great white shark is an example of a pelagic shark. Some sharks prefer to live on the ocean floor – they are called benthic sharks. A wobbegong is a benthic shark. Other sharks live close to the surface. The illustration below shows where some sharks live in the ocean.

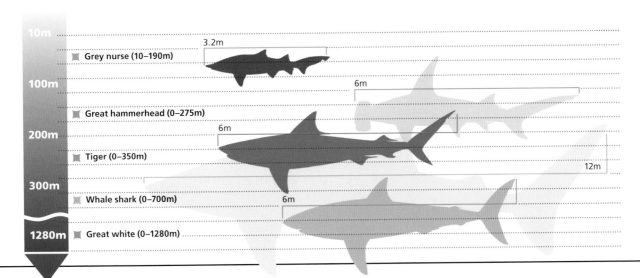

10m

■ Grey nurse (10–190m)   3.2m

100m   6m

■ Great hammerhead (0–275m)

200m   6m

■ Tiger (0–350m)   12m

300m

■ Whale shark (0–700m)   6m

1280m ■ Great white (0–1280m)

GOBBLE TROUBLE

In the ocean, sharks are apex predators. This means that it is very rare that another animal will catch and kill a shark. They are at the top of the food chain. Animals at the top of the food chain play a very important role in keeping populations of other animals in balance.

FEROCIOUS FACT!

WHO MUNCHES WHO?

A food chain is a way of showing who eats who in a certain environment. Here are two examples of food chains in the ocean. As you can see, there is a shark at the top of both of them.

BLACKTIP REEF SHARKS EAT PARROTFISH. PARROTFISH EAT CORAL.

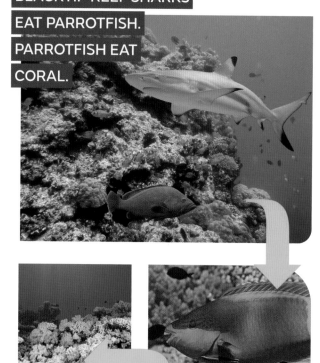

TIGER SHARKS EAT LOGGERHEAD TURTLES. LOGGERHEAD TURTLES EAT SQUID. SQUID EAT SHRIMP.

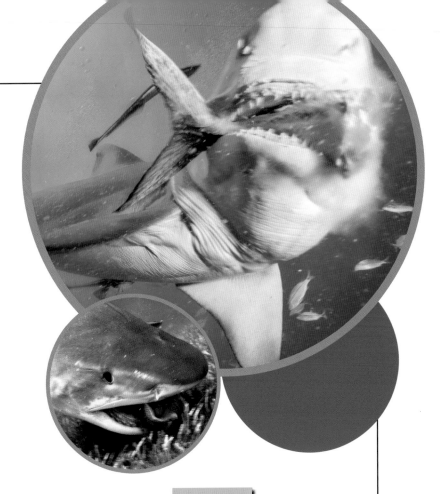

WHAT'S ON THE MENU?

All sharks are carnivorous, which means they eat other animals. Sharks eat a huge variety of animals. Fast-moving predators such as the tiger shark, bull shark and great hammerhead shark feast on everything from fish, crustaceans and squid, to sea lions, smaller sharks and seals. Some sharks even eat birds, sneaking up on them from beneath the water's surface!

Slow-moving, bottom-dwelling sharks such as the wobbegong and zebra shark eat crustaceans, molluscs and other shellfish.

Filter feeders eat tiny marine animals like krill and plankton – which is funny because filter feeders are the largest sharks! Examples of filter feeders include whale sharks and basking sharks.

BASKING SHARK

? DID YOU KNOW?

Sharks don't drink water through their mouths. Instead, they filter sea water through their gills.

Q & A

Q: Can you fill in the blanks on this food chain?

G_____ white sharks eat _____. Seals eat _____. Squid eat krill. _____ eat plankton.

A: Great; seals; squid ; krill

GREY NURSE SHARK

DEADLY FACTOR:

4/10

Fact File

OTHER NAMES: Spotted ragged-tooth shark, sand tiger shark, blue nurse sand tiger shark.

LENGTH: Up to 3.2m.

DIET: Fish, squid, crabs and other sharks.

DISTRIBUTION: All parts of Australia except Tasmania, though rare in the Northern Territory.

HABITAT: Tropical and temperate water. It spends most of its time on the ocean floor, but also spends some time just below the water's surface.

BREEDING: Mature female grey nurse sharks give birth to two live pups about once a year.

TRUE OR FALSE?

While they're still growing inside their mother, baby grey nurse sharks eat each other until there is only one left.

A: True

SCARY TEETH

Even though the grey nurse shark has rows of sharp, scary-looking teeth, it is actually quite calm and not dangerous to humans. The reason it has such sharp teeth is so it can grab and hold onto its prey.

FEROCIOUS FACT!

The grey nurse shark is vulnerable to extinction, which means there are not many left in the ocean. Because of overfishing they are at risk of being wiped out. Because they don't give birth to many pups, it will take a long time for their numbers to get back to a safe level.

DID YOU KNOW?

The grey nurse shark will poke its head out of the water and swallow air into its stomach. This helps it stay buoyant.

SHARK SUPERPOWERS

Sharks have been around since before dinosaurs walked the earth! It takes a very well-designed animal to survive such a long time. Sharks have developed some amazing abilities to help them become the top predators in the ocean.

SIGHT

Although sharks can't see as far as they can smell or hear, they still have excellent sight in the water. Most sharks can see better in dim light than their prey. A great white, for example, swims very low in the water and searches for the outline of its prey close to the surface. By the time the prey has realised the shark is there, it's already too late!

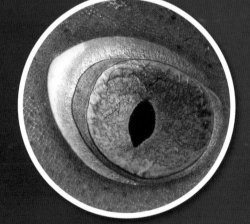

VIBRATIONS

Sharks can also sense movement or vibrations in the water, using a special system of vessels that run underneath their skin. That's why sharks are attracted to animals, including humans and dogs, that are kicking or splashing in the water.

SMELL

A shark has an incredible sense of smell, particularly for blood, which it can sense from a long way away. Sharks can identify the equivalent of one teaspoonful of blood in an Olympic-sized swimming pool!

ELECTRICAL SIGNALS

Sharks have one super sense that humans don't have – they can pick up electrical signals. This is called electroreception. All animals, even tiny ones, give off electrical signals when they move. Sharks pick up these signals using tiny receptors in their snouts. The great hammerhead shark, which has a very big and wide snout, has more receptors than any other shark, so it can pick up electrical signals the best.

HEARING

Instead of having ears like ours, a shark has a tiny hole on either side of its head. These shark ears can pick up sounds from many kilometres away. They hear low-pitched sounds the best and can pick up sounds that are too low for humans to hear.

TIGER SHARK

DEADLY FACTOR: 7/10

Fact File

LENGTH: Up to 6m.

DIET: Fishes, cephalopods, birds, crustaceans, reptiles, mammals.

DISTRIBUTION: From Windy Harbour, Western Australia, north along the coast to Sydney, New South Wales.

HABITAT: Coastal, mainly tropical waters from surface to 150m down.

BREEDING: Female tiger sharks give birth to between 10 and 80 pups, which are usually up to 76cm long.

FEROCIOUS FACT!

This is one of the largest sharks in the world. Although adults are usually no more than 3-4m long, they can grow to more than 7m. When they reach this size they can weigh almost a tonne.

CURIOSITY CAN KILL

It's probably because they've got such a wide-ranging diet that tiger sharks are very curious creatures. Rather than being scared of an unknown object in the water, they'll swim up and bite it out of curiosity. Unfortunately, when a big shark does this to a human, the injuries can be fatal.

DID YOU KNOW?

Tiger shark mothers give birth to live babies and there can be more than 80 pups in one litter!

I EAT EVERYTHING!

This fish will eat almost anything – from normal shark food, like turtles and fish, to more unusual snacks, like bags of rubbish and bits of cars dumped in the ocean. Combine that habit with a big body size, and you get one of the few sharks known to have attacked and killed humans.

TRICKS OF THE TRADE

Different sharks have developed some very useful behaviours and tricks to help them travel, hunt and feed.

◄ Fin feet

No, sharks don't have any feet! But some sharks, such as the whitetip reef shark (left) or epaulette shark, can fold their dorsal fins over and use their pectoral fins to 'walk' forwards or backwards when hunting in small spaces.

THE ORGANS THAT HELP THESE SHARKS GLOW ARE CALLED PHOTOPHORES.

▼ Cookie monster

Look at the shape of this cookie-cutter shark's mouth. It's specially designed for feeding. First, the shark opens its mouth wide and attaches it onto the surface of its prey. Then it swivels its body around so that its teeth cut out a round, cookie-shaped piece of flesh or blubber. This does not kill the animal they are feeding on.

▲ Invisibility shield

Lanternsharks have a very clever way of hiding from predators and prey. They have special organs in the skin on its belly that glow in the dark. Anything below a lanternshark thinks it is just looking at the sun shining down through the water. They can't see the shark at all!

▶ Keeping cool vs staying warm.

Most fish, including sharks, are cold-blooded. They can't control the temperature of their bodies, so they have the same body temperature as the water they are swimming in. The great white shark, however, can keep its body temperature steady no matter the temperature of the water. This is why great white sharks are such effective predators in a wide range of water temperatures.

▲ Freshwater shark

While most sharks only live in the ocean, where the water is salty, the bull shark can survive in fresh water, too. This is because it can adjust its kidneys to suit different levels of salt in the water. Bull sharks can therefore swim up rivers, a long way from the ocean. Pretty clever!

WHALE SHARK

Fact File

LENGTH: Up to 12m.

DIET: Plankton, small crustaceans and fishes, sometimes squid.

DISTRIBUTION: Mainly off the northern coastline from Exmouth, Western Australia to Queensland.

HABITAT: Tropical and warm water, anywhere from the surface to very deep in the ocean.

BREEDING: Whale sharks give birth to live young. No one has seen a whale shark give birth, and no one knows how often it happens.

DEADLY FACTOR: 1/10

DID YOU KNOW?

A whale shark's skin is about 15cm thick. That's about three times as thick as your wrist!

SPOT THE DIFFERENCE

Each whale shark has a unique pattern of spots on its skin. No two whale sharks have the same pattern. This has helped scientists to identify, count and keep track of whale sharks around the world. This in turn helps us to protect these magnificent animals.

TRUE OR FALSE?

Whale sharks are harmless, so it's okay to swim up and touch one.

Answer:
FALSE

Although they're harmless, whale sharks are sensitive animals and should be treated with respect. Boats and swimmers should keep a safe distance.

FEROCIOUS FACT!

The whale shark is a shark and NOT a whale. People call it a whale shark because it's so big, like a whale.

BIG APPETITE FOR TINY FISH

Even though the whale shark is the biggest fish in the ocean, it likes to eat food like plankton and krill. That means it has to eat a lot of them! It feeds by sucking huge amounts of water in through its massive mouth and out through its gills. As the water passes through, the tiny fish get caught in special filters at the back of the shark's mouth.

SHARK BABIES

Sharks are pretty secretive when it comes to giving birth – not many people have ever seen it happen, or even seen a newborn shark baby. This secrecy and protection is another reason why sharks are top survivors in the ocean.

FEROCIOUS FACT!

THIS FEMALE SHARK HAS SCARS FROM MATING.

HOW DO SHARKS BREED?

Unlike bony fishes, sharks' eggs are fertilised inside the female's body. A male shark has special organs, called 'claspers', on the underside of his body, which he uses to latch on to the female to fertilise her eggs. During mating, the male often bites the female on her back and fins to help him get into the right position.

Most sharks give birth to live young, but some sharks – like the Port Jackson shark – lay eggs, which are left among seaweed or wedged into rocks.

When the baby shark is born, it already has a full set of teeth! Most sharks are born ready to swim away and start hunting. They don't need their parents to look after them.

The number of babies born depends on the type of shark. Some species only give birth to one or two babies. Others can give birth to up to 100 babies at a time.

The amount of time the baby takes to develop inside the mother (known as the gestation period) also depends on the species. The gestation period for sharks ranges from about nine months (which is the same as a human baby) to as long as two years.

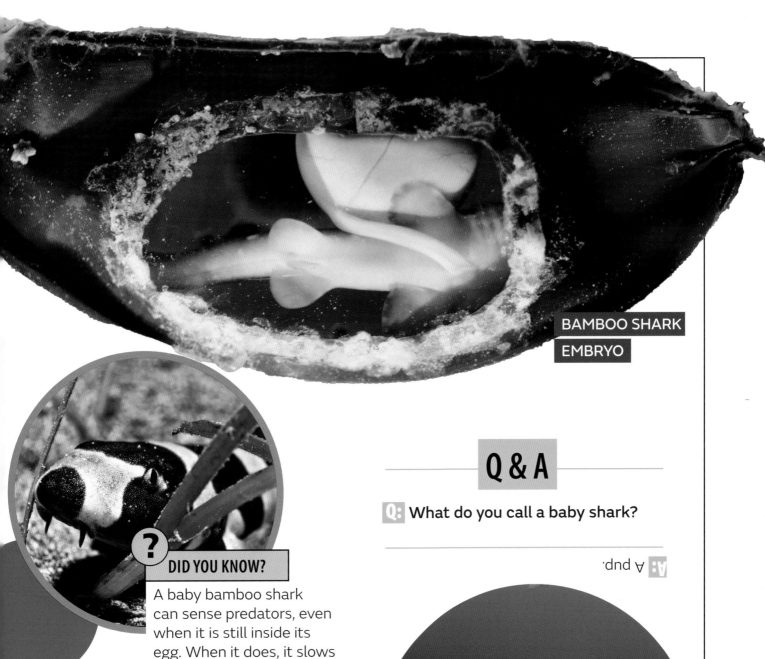

BAMBOO SHARK
EMBRYO

? DID YOU KNOW?

A baby bamboo shark can sense predators, even when it is still inside its egg. When it does, it slows its body right down and pretends that it is dead, so that the predator isn't tempted to try and eat it.

FEROCIOUS FACT!

In some cases, the embryos (baby sharks) compete and eat each other inside the mother. They do this because they need nourishment to help them survive and grow, so their natural instinct is to eat their brothers or sisters in order to ensure their own survival.

Q & A

Q: What do you call a baby shark?

A: A pup.

IT'S A MYSTERY!

Nobody has ever seen whale sharks mate or give birth. In fact, no one really knows how many babies a whale shark can give birth to. Only one pregnant whale shark has ever been seen.

WOBBEGONGS

Fact File

OTHER NAMES: Carpet shark.

LENGTH: Up to 3m.

DIET: Small fishes, crabs, crayfish and octopuses.

DISTRIBUTION: Mostly found in Pacific waters, though different species can be found all around the Australian coast.

HABITAT: Shallow waters. They spend most of their time on the seabed.

BREEDING: Wobbegongs breed only once every three years. They give birth to large numbers of live pups.

◄ Sneaky

The wobbegong is an ambush predator. This means that instead of actively hunting its prey, the wobbegong lies still on the ocean floor and waits for prey to approach. When the time is right, it lunges with lightning-fast reflexes and snags the fish in its sharp teeth.

FISH, CHIPS AND LEATHER

Although wobbegongs don't eat humans, humans eat wobbegongs! Wobbegong meat is popular in fish and chip shops. Their skin is also used to make leather.

TRUE OR FALSE?

If you grab a wobbegong by the tail, it can't bite you.

Answer:
FALSE

These sharks are very flexible, and could easily swing around and catch your hand. Better leave it alone!

FEROCIOUS FACT!

There are 10 different species of wobbegong. Most of them are found in Australian waters.

WEIRD AND WONDERFUL

A selection of some of the most unusual sharks from around the world.

▶ Basking shark

This is the second-largest living shark, after the whale shark. Like the whale shark, it feeds on tiny fish by sucking water in through its mouth, catching the fish in filters at the back of its mouth, then pushing the water back out through its gills. Its big nose has led to one of its other names – the elephant shark.

◀ Angelshark

This shark looks more like a ray than a shark. It has a really flat body and large pectoral fins. The colour of its skin allows it to blend in with the ocean floor and hide from its prey. When something tasty comes close, the angelshark suddenly bursts forward and quickly snaps it up.

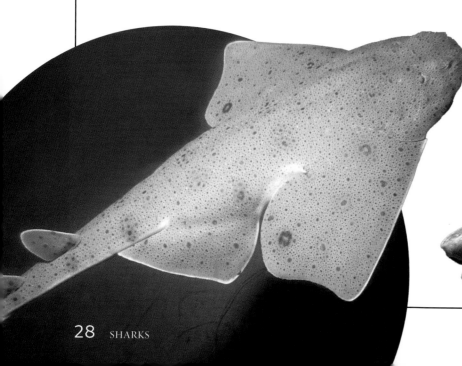

▲ Goblin shark

With an extremely long snout, long jaws and pinkish body, the goblin shark is one very strange-looking shark! It lives in the very deep parts of the ocean, where there's no sunlight. That means it can't see its prey – instead, it picks up on their electrical signals. When it gets close, it sucks its prey in to its mouth and then gobbles it up!

▼ Frilled shark

This shark looks like a cross between a snake, an eel and a lizard. It grows to about 2m, or as long as a door. It is a very rare shark that usually swims in the deep ocean. It has big gill slits, which look like frills around its neck. It also has lots and lots of sharp teeth, which it uses to bite into squid and small fish.

▲ Sawshark

No prizes for guessing where this shark got its name from! The longnose sawshark's nose is like a big saw, with teeth running along the edges. It cruises along the sea floor, and when it finds its prey, it swings its nose from side to side, whacking and crippling its prey.

BULL SHARK

Fact File

OTHER NAMES: River whaler, freshwater whaler.

WEIGHT: 100-200kg.

DIET: Mainly fishes, small sharks and rays, dolphins, turtles, birds and molluscs.

DISTRIBUTION: Along the northern coast between Perth, Western Australia and Sydney, New South Wales.

HABITAT: Shallow waters along coasts and up into freshwater rivers.

BREEDING: A female bull shark gives birth to between 1–13 live young at once, often near lagoons or river mouths. Newborns are about 70cm long and survive independently after birth.

DEADLY FACTOR:

9/10

TRUE OR FALSE?

Bull sharks have been known to attack and kill people swimming in waist-deep water.

A: True

MAN-KILLER!

Very few shark species deserve the label 'man-killer', but this is a rare exception. It's one of three shark species responsible for most attacks on people in Australia and worldwide; the other two are great white and tiger sharks.

FEROCIOUS FACT!

A bull shark hunts where we swim — around the coast and in harbours and bays. Unlike other sharks, it even goes well up into freshwater rivers.

DID YOU KNOW?

In the past 100 years there have been over 150 fatal shark attacks in Australian waters. About 1/3 have been in NSW, as more people swim there.

FORMER NAVY DIVER PAUL DE GELDER WAS ATTACKED IN 2009. HE IS NOW A SUPPORTER OF SHARK CONSERVATION.

WHO'S SCARIER: THEM OR US?

It's true that sharks can sometimes attack humans, causing serious injury or even death. But there are also lots of ways that humans can injure or kill sharks. In many ways, sharks have more to fear from us than we do from them.

THREATS TO SHARKS

Fishing

Large numbers of sharks are caught each year. Individual fishers like the challenge of catching a shark, while big fishing companies, called fisheries, catch sharks to sell. A fisher may often kill a shark without knowing it. Lots of sharks will get away when they bite and swallow the hook. The hook gets caught inside them, causing them to get sick and die.

▲ Shark finning

One way that humans hunt sharks is by cutting off their fins and allowing the shark to return to the sea. Shark fins are expensive and are used in a popular dish called shark fin soup. They are also a symbol of class and status in Chinese culture. Sharks that have their fins cut off cannot swim properly and will often die of blood loss or suffocation.

▼ Bycatch

Another big cause of shark deaths is when they are accidentally caught by fisheries who are targeting another species. This is called bycatch.

▼ Shark nets

Shark nets are nets that are put up just off the coast of swimming beaches in Australia, to stop sharks from entering and attacking swimmers. Unfortunately, sharks sometimes get tangled up in these nets and drown.

Big bite!

Rodney Fox is lucky to have survived when a great white shark attacked him off the coast of South Australia in 1963. He needed 465 stitches. Far from being afraid of sharks, Rodney went on to fight hard for their protection.

? DID YOU KNOW?

More than 100 million sharks worldwide are killed by humans each year. That is a LOT of sharks. Shark populations are dropping very quickly, and some shark species are in danger of disappearing altogether.

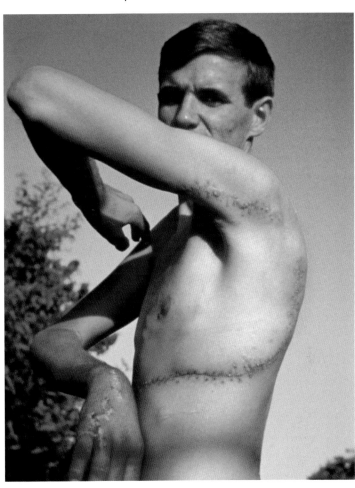

STEER CLEAR OF SHARKS

Here are five tips for shark-safe swimming:

1. Swim at beaches that are patrolled by surf lifesavers.
2. Do not swim in areas known for dangerous sharks.
3. Avoid swimming or surfing alone.
4. Avoid swimming or surfing at dawn, dusk or night. These are typically the feeding times for a lot of sharks.
5. Check deep water carefully before jumping in from a boat.

SNAKE PEEK

Snakes are reptiles which means they are cold-blooded, lay eggs and have scales. All snakes are carnivorous which means they mostly eat meat. Snakes might appear scary, but they're actually pretty amazing!

FEROCIOUS FACT!

The scales on a snake are incredibly useful. They help to protect the snake and stop it from drying out. Scales help the snake to move smoothly without using too much energy. They may look slimy, but they are actually quite dry. Some snakes are very smooth, while others feel rough.

DID YOU KNOW?

Snakes have something called a Jacobson's organ. Their tongue picks up chemicals in the air and passes them to this organ, which helps them to track prey.

GOOD GLOTTIS

When we have a mouth full of food, we can only breathe through our noses. A snake can still breathe through its mouth when it is eating because its windpipe (glottis) sticks out of the bottom of its mouth.

ROUGH-SCALED SNAKE

▼ Pit

Some snakes have special pits behind their nostrils which they use to sense temperature changes in the air around them. This helps them to track down the warm bodies of their prey.

▶ Fang

▶ Glottis

▶ Tongue

The flicking, forked tongue picks up tiny particles in the air which tell the snake everything about its surroundings. Snakes are very good at using their tongues to 'smell' what is going on around them.

▼ Nostril

A snake only uses its nostrils for breathing, not for smelling. It uses its tongue for smelling.

▼ Eyes

Snakes don't have eyelids; instead they have a clear scale covering each eye. This protects the eye from damage.

▼ Venom gland

This is where the venom is produced. Not all snakes have venom. Venom is a kind of poisonous saliva which travels through the fangs and is injected into prey to kill or stun.

WARMING UP

Snakes are cold-blooded which means their body temperature depends on the environment around them. Snakes need to be warm in order to move or digest food, so they sometimes bask in the sun. If it is too hot they find somewhere cool to hide.

FEROCIOUS FACT!

Snakes don't have eardrums. They 'hear' by picking up on low frequency vibrations in the air and on the ground.

A Snake's LIFE

All snakes go through the same life cycle. The only big difference is that some snakes lay eggs, while others give birth to live young.

Eggs

If it is an egg-laying snake, the female will lay her eggs in a moist place where the sun can help keep them at the right temperature. Some snakes, such as the water python, coil around their eggs to keep them warm. The number of eggs depends on the type of snake. Some snakes lay only a few; others as many as 100 eggs at one time.

Hatchlings

The length of time it takes for the eggs to hatch depends on the species and the temperature of the eggs. It can take as long as a couple of months. The baby snake uses a special tooth, called an egg tooth, to help it break out of its shell. It loses this tooth soon after hatching.

DID YOU KNOW?

Baby snakes are left on their own after they are born and are perfect prey for predators. Less than one in 10 newborn snakes survive.

▸ Live young

Some snakes, like the red-bellied black snake and the tiger snake, give birth to live young. This can happen in two different ways. Either a mother nourishes the baby inside her body until it is born, or they are hatched inside the mother and are born alive.

▼ Mating

Snakes usually mate in spring when the cold weather is over. The male will move over the female, rubbing her body with his chin. Sometimes the male and female get all twisted up together, like a piece of liquorice!

Q & A

Q: **How long do snakes live?**

A: It depends on the species – some snakes will only live a couple of years, while others will live for up to 25 years.

FEROCIOUS FACT!

Snakes don't like cold weather because it makes them slow down. In really cold places, snakes hibernate through winter. This means they find a safe place and go into a type of deep sleep. This helps them save energy and survive for a long time without food. When it gets warmer, they come out of their hiding place and go hunting for food.

▲ Shedding

As they grow, snakes shed their skin. This is also called moulting. Young snakes moult more often than older snakes because they are growing more quickly. When a snake is just about to moult, the scales over its eyes turn light blue. Once the skin is shed, the snake's eyes go back to their normal colour. The snake's skin peels off in one piece like a sock. Underneath is a clean, fresh skin that fits perfectly!

RED -BELLIED BLACK SNAKE

Fact File

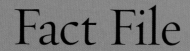

FOUND: Along the eastern coast of Australia.

LIVES: In burrows, hollow logs and beneath rocks in places where there is access to water.

DIET: Mainly frogs, but also lizards, mammals, birds and fish.

BREEDING: Gives birth to up to 40 live young at a time.

LENGTH: Up to 1.5 metres.

DEADLY FACTOR:

9/10

DID YOU KNOW?
Red-bellied black snakes will eat canned dog food!

ALTHOUGH IT IS DANGEROUSLY VENOMOUS, THE RED-BELLIED BLACK SNAKE IS SHY AND UNLIKELY TO BITE. INSTEAD, IT WILL PUT ON A SCARY DISPLAY, HISSING AND FLATTENING ITS NECK AGGRESSIVELY.

SKILLED SWIMMERS

These snakes are just as happy hunting in water as they are on land. They like to eat fish and tadpoles as well as land-based animals. They can even feed underwater.

FEROCIOUS FACT!

During breeding season, males will fight each other for the right to mate with a female. Fighting males twist around each other and try to pin the other down. Sometimes they will bite each other, although they are immune to their own venom. The fight will last up to half an hour, with the loser leaving the area.

SWALLOW THIS

Snakes are mostly very slender and have quite small heads, and yet they are capable of eating quite large animals. How do they do it?

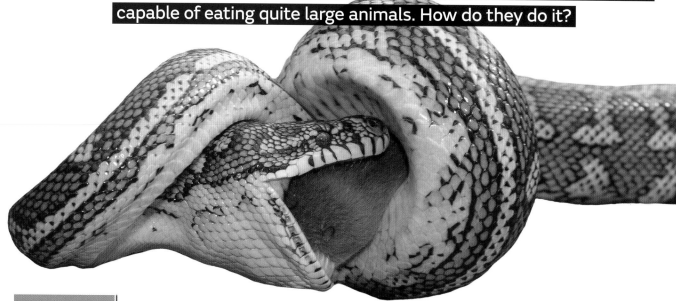

MEATY MENU

All snakes are carnivorous which means they only eat other animals. This includes smaller animals such as insects, mice, lizards, frogs, other snakes, snails and eggs, as well as much bigger animals such as birds, cats and chickens. Although they are very narrow, snakes can fit a lot of differently sized animals inside their bodies.

UNBELIEVABLE

Pythons are so big that they can crush big animals and slowly consume them. Pythons have even been known to eat goats. The olive python in the photo below is swallowing a rock wallaby.

DID YOU KNOW?

The bandy-bandy is a snake that only eats one type of small snake called a blind snake. It is known to eat blind snakes that are the same size as itself!

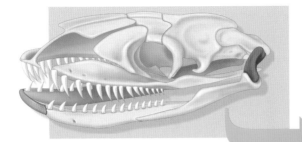
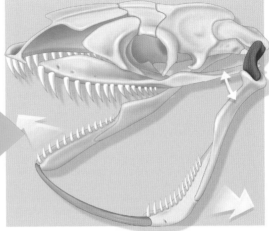

The secret to a snake's big meal lies in its jaw. A snake can separate the top and bottom parts of its jaw which means it can open its mouth really wide. It can also stretch its head, throat and skin. This way it can swallow its prey whole. Once inside, strong juices in the snake's stomach dissolve the prey's body.

IN THE POO

Snakes can't digest fur or feathers, beaks or eggshells. This stuff comes out the other end as snake poo. Snake poo is mushy, messy and usually dark brown. Sometimes it has a streak of white in it.

AFTER LUNCH NAP

After eating, a snake needs its energy to digest, so it becomes dormant. The amount of time it takes to finish digesting depends on the size of the snake, the size of its meal and the temperature of its surroundings. Snakes don't need to eat very often, particularly after a big meal.

TRUE OR FALSE?

Snakes drink water.

A: True

Venom vs constriction

Venomous snakes bite their prey first. Some parts of the venom paralyse the prey so it can't get away. Other compounds inside the venom help with the process of digestion. Non-venomous snakes use constriction, tightening their own bodies around their prey until blood flow is stopped and the animal dies.

Q & A

Q: Can a snake swallow a human?

A: Although there are a couple of species of snake that are capable of swallowing an adult human, it is extremely rare.

WHERE DO SNAKES LIVE?

Snakes live all over the world! Whether it's desert or rainforest, flat or mountainous, grassy or rocky – snakes have figured out a way to survive there. Here we explore the different types of places that snakes live in Australia.

◀ Deserts

The desert areas of Australia are very dry and can get very hot during the day. Snakes that live in these places will often shelter under rocks, in cracks in the ground, or in burrows until the temperature drops and they can go out hunting. The woma python is a snake that lives in Australian deserts. It often takes shelter in rabbit burrows during the day and only hunts at night.

▶ Forests

Snakes love forests because there are plenty of animals to eat and plenty of places to find shelter and protection. Quite a few snakes like to live and hunt in trees, like this amethystine python. Its tail is specially designed to help it grip onto branches and move through trees. Other good places for snakes that live in forests are in hollow logs, under fallen tree branches and under dead leaves lying on the ground. The black-striped snake is one species that takes shelter on the ground. It likes to eat small lizards.

DID YOU KNOW?
The female amethystine python is usually longer and heavier than the male.

▲ Oceans

There are lots of snakes that spend time in the water. In fact, some snakes don't ever leave the ocean and give birth to live young underwater, such as this olive sea snake.

▶ Mountains

Snakes don't really like the cold, so there are only a few species that live in the mountains in Australia, where the weather is much cooler. The highland copperhead snake is one species that doesn't mind lower temperatures. Snakes that live in cool places in Australia generally give birth to live young because eggs would not survive the cold.

▼ Waterways

Snakes are good swimmers, and some snakes spend their whole lives in water. File snakes, like the Arafura file snake, live in rivers and billabongs in northern Australia. They eat fish, catching them by biting them and then gripping on to them with their rough skin.

▲ Grasslands

Grasslands are flat, open places that are mainly covered with grass. They provide shelter for many different animals, including snakes. This collared whip snake likes grasslands, where it feeds mainly on lizards. Other examples of snakes living in grasslands are brown snakes and tiger snakes.

PYTHONS

Fact File

FOUND: In countries where there is plenty of warm weather and water, including Australia.

LIVES: In caves or trees, also cities and towns.

DIET: Small animals such as lizards, birds, mammals, rodents, and larger animals like pigs, goats, cats and chickens.

BREEDING: Egg-laying.

LENGTH: Shortest is 60 centimetres; longest 9 metres.

HOLD ME TIGHT

Pythons are constrictors which means they kill their prey by squeezing them to death. Pythons wrap their strong bodies around their prey and squeeze so tightly that blood can no longer flow to their organs, and the prey dies. Then they uncoil themselves and swallow their prey whole.

GREEN TREE PYTHON

LOVELY AND LONG

This beautiful snake is a carpet python. It is found across most of Australia and can grow very long – about as long as two grown men lying end to end!

WARM HUGS

A mother python keeps her eggs warm by coiling around them and shivering her muscles.

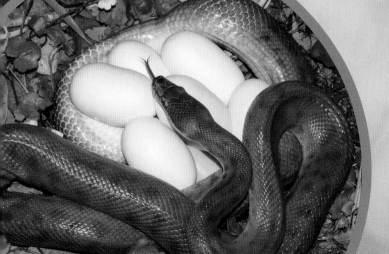

FEROCIOUS FACT!

There are about 20 types of python in Australia. They come in a huge range of colours, shapes and sizes. Many of them are very beautiful. Although they grow quite big and heavy, they are non-venomous and are generally quite and peaceful around humans, which is why they are popular pets.

SLITHERIN'

Most snakes move by slithering along the ground.
But did you know there's more than one way to slither?
There are four basic ways a snake moves:

▼ Serpentine This is the most common way snakes move, and probably what you picture when you think of a snake slithering. The snake forms an 'S' shape with its body and pushes against things on the ground such as grass, rocks and twigs to move forward.

▼ Sidewinding Some snakes, travelling across surfaces such as sand or mud, use a motion called sidewinding. The snake lifts most of its body off the ground and launches itself sideways. It looks a little bit like the snake is jumping sideways across the ground.

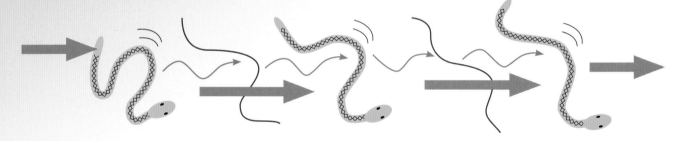

▼ Caterpillar This is just what it sounds like – the snake moves the same way as a caterpillar. Instead of its body making curves from side to side, its curves are up and down. This is useful if the snake is in a tight space that doesn't allow it to curve sideways.

▼ Concertina If a snake wants to climb vertically, up a tree trunk for example, it uses the concertina movement. First it stretches its head and front of body forward, then it bunches the middle of its body up and uses its belly scales to get a grip on the tree. It then brings its back end and tail up. By doing this over and over, the snake will slowly climb the tree.

FEROCIOUS FACT!

It's true — some snakes can fly! A flying snake will launch itself off a tree branch, flatten its body and glide through the air, kind of like a Frisbee. They can't fly upwards like birds can, but they can travel up to 100 metres, which is as long as a football field! Unfortunately these snakes don't live in Australia — you would have to travel to South East Asia, China or India to see a snake fly.

ATTACK AND DEFENCE

Snakes have spent millions of years perfecting their skills for capturing prey and staying alive. Here are some of the ways snakes hunt and protect themselves.

HIDE AND STRIKE

Some snakes will lie in wait at a spot where prey is likely to be – for example, under a rock where lizards like to sun themselves, or in a tree that attracts birds or mammals. When the prey comes within reach...WHAM! The snake strikes out and catches its prey by surprise. This method of hunting is called an ambush.

CAN'T SEE ME!

Camouflage is a very useful tool for snakes. It helps them hunt and keeps them safe from predators because the colour and pattern on their skin blends in with their background. You can see how this green tree snake blends into the rainforest where it lives. It even has white spots that look like sunlight filtering through leaves.

WORM WRIGGLE

Ever noticed how the tip of a snake's tail looks like a worm? Some snakes, like the Australian death adder, use this to their advantage. They hide and wiggle the end of their tail just like a worm. When a hungry bird or mammal comes in for a taste, it gets a very nasty surprise!

ON THE PROWL

Some snakes actively hunt for their food. They use their amazing sense of smell to track down animals that might be sleeping in burrows. The yellow-faced whip snake even cruises around until it spots an animal such as a lizard, then chases it.

FEROCIOUS FACT!

Some snakes use pretty clever tricks to stay safe. Hognose snakes, from North and South America, pretend to be dead when they sense trouble. Their predators prefer live animals, so they leave them alone. Another American trickster, the milk snake, is harmless, but it copies the colours of venomous snakes, which scares predators away.

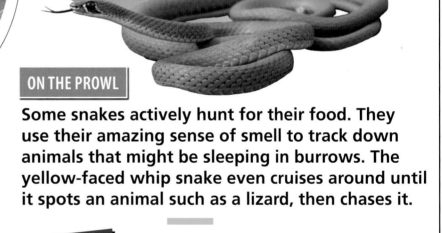

GWARDAR

DEADLY FACTOR:

9/10

Fact File

FOUND: Across most of Australia.

LIVES: Likes hiding under things like fallen tree branches or rocks, piles of rubbish or building materials, and in burrows and cracks in the ground.

DIET: Lizards, birds, mice and other small animals.

BREEDING: Lays about 20 eggs at a time.

LENGTH: Up to 1.8 metres.

FEROCIOUS FACT!

The gwardar is very quick, which might explain why humans don't often see it. When it strikes, it holds on to its prey, and sometimes wraps its body around it to make absolutely sure it won't lose its dinner!

This is one of Australia's most widespread and deadly snakes, but it rarely bothers humans...phew! It's a type of brown snake which makes it very venomous. It comes in a range of colours and patterns including orange with a black head and light brown with thick black stripes.

SHARP EYES

While most snakes rely on their sense of smell to track prey, the gwardar has very good eyesight and will often spot its dinner rather than smell it.

DID YOU KNOW?

The gwardar prefers to hunt during the day, but if the weather is very hot, it will wait until the afternoon or evening to get out and about.

COLOUR CHANGE

The gwardar can change colour with the season.

MOST VENOMOUS

Each year up to 3000 people are bitten by snakes in Australia! These days, because of effective antivenoms, usually only one or two snakebite victims die each year. These are some of Australia's most venomous snakes.

DEADLY FACTOR:

8/10

▸ Eastern brown snake

No other snake species bites or kills more people in Australia than the eastern brown snake. Brown snake venom contains an exceptionally strong and fast-acting nerve toxin, although compared to many other snakes, their small fangs don't inject much venom when they bite. This is the snake you're most likely to come into contact with in Australia. It's an agile snake that becomes very aggressive when cornered - so be careful if you meet one!

FEROCIOUS FACT!

A polyvalent antivenom is now available — it works on the bites of all Australian snakes, although it is still best to use the antivenom specifically designed for each species. You should never wash a snakebite wound because the venom left around it can be used to identify the type of snake that caused the injury.

DID YOU KNOW?

If disturbed, the eastern brown raises its body off the ground, winding into an 'S' shape, mouth gaping open and ready to strike.

Common death adder

This snake has such toxic venom that it's on the list of the top 10 deadliest snakes in the world! Death adders don't move about much, but prefer to lie hidden waiting for prey. They have one of the fastest strikes of any snake and are a common hazard for bushwalkers.

Dugite (spotted brown snake)

This highly venomous snake is active during the daytime and often seen around urban and semi-rural areas. The species is particularly well-known to Perth residents; it's responsible for three-quarters of all snakebite admissions to hospitals in the area. Without antivenom, there's a high chance that a bite can be fatal, although the actual bite itself is said to be almost painless with no real swelling.

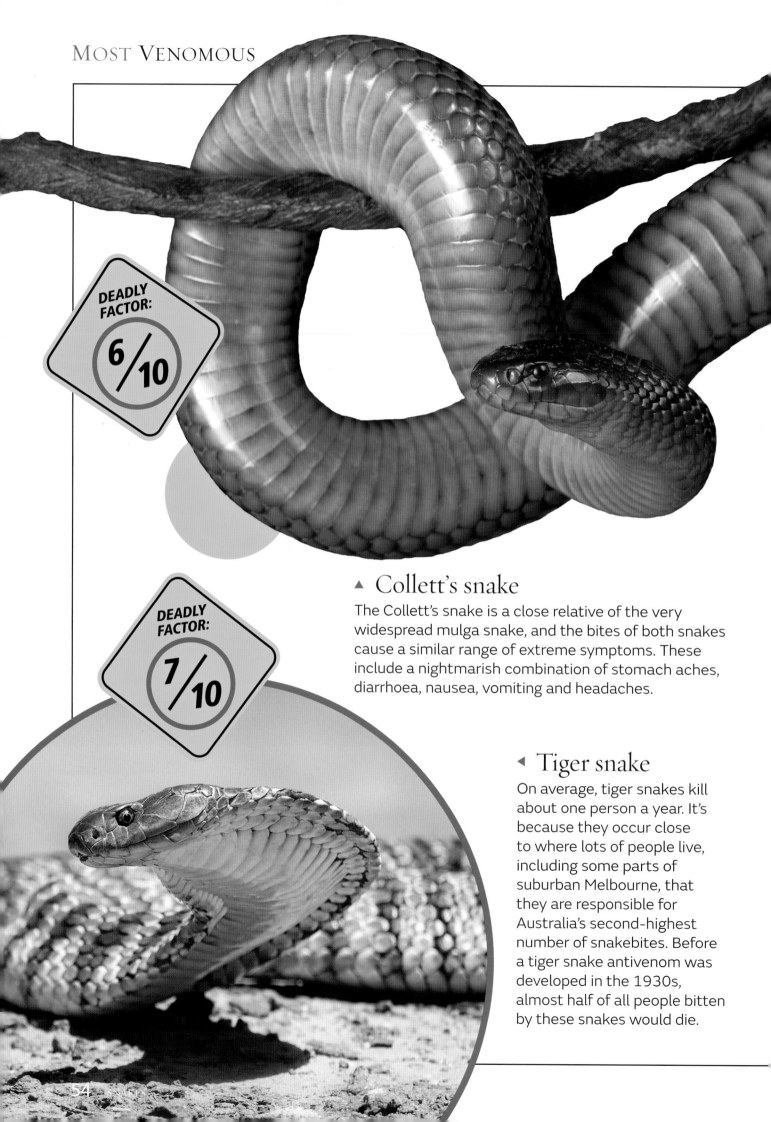

DEADLY FACTOR:

6/10

▲ Collett's snake

The Collett's snake is a close relative of the very widespread mulga snake, and the bites of both snakes cause a similar range of extreme symptoms. These include a nightmarish combination of stomach aches, diarrhoea, nausea, vomiting and headaches.

DEADLY FACTOR:

7/10

◄ Tiger snake

On average, tiger snakes kill about one person a year. It's because they occur close to where lots of people live, including some parts of suburban Melbourne, that they are responsible for Australia's second-highest number of snakebites. Before a tiger snake antivenom was developed in the 1930s, almost half of all people bitten by these snakes would die.

▸ Inland taipan

A high-potency mix of killer compounds makes the inland taipan the world's most venomous snake – it could kill an adult in 45 minutes. However, the inland taipan is not the most dangerous snake in the world. That's because this snake only lives in a very isolated part of the country, and also has a shy and laid-back temperament.

DEADLY FACTOR:

6/10

DEADLY FACTOR:

7/10

▾ Coastal taipan

The coastal taipan is the third most toxic snake in the world, and it has the longest fangs of any Australian snake – about 13mm long, meaning it can deliver a serious bite. Before the introduction of its antivenom in 1956, taipan bites were nearly always fatal. In severe cases, death can occur in just 30 minutes. An extremely alert and nervous creature, it prefers to avoid confrontation but puts up a ferocious defence if cornered or surprised. First it stops still, and then hurls its lightweight body forward.

DEADLY FACTOR:

7/10

▴ Mulga (king brown)

This snake's biggest claim to fame is that it produces more venom than any other snake in the world when it bites. It can deliver a massive 150mg of venom when it strikes – as much as four times more than other venomous snakes. When they bite, they hang on and chew!

SNAKEBITE SAFETY

As long as you know how to avoid getting bitten by a snake, and what to do in case you are, you can stay safe!

PLEASE BE AWARE OF SNAKES IN WARMER MONTHS

How does venom work?

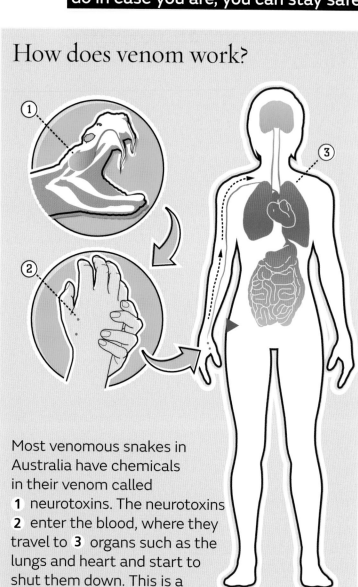

Most venomous snakes in Australia have chemicals in their venom called **1** neurotoxins. The neurotoxins **2** enter the blood, where they travel to **3** organs such as the lungs and heart and start to shut them down. This is a very effective way of bringing down an animal that might be much larger or stronger than the snake. Unfortunately, the venom works on humans in the same way. This is why venomous snakes in Australia are so dangerous to humans.

FIGHT OR FLIGHT

The main reason snakes bite is to get food. Venomous snakes will strike and inject venom into their prey to kill or immobilise it and make it easier to eat. Non-venomous snakes will bite to grab hold of their prey. The other reason snakes bite is for defence. Snakes are generally not aggressive; they will try to escape first and will only bite if they feel threatened.

FEROCIOUS FACT!

Antivenom is a medicine that is injected into someone who has been bitten by a venomous snake. The antivenom stops the body from reacting to the snake's venom. Thankfully, there are antivenoms for most of Australia's dangerous snakes, so as long as you get to a doctor or hospital quickly, you can be treated.

STEER CLEAR

There are a few things you can do to lower your chances of being bitten by a snake.

Wear snake-proof clothing. If you're in a place where you think there might be snakes, wear closed shoes, thick socks and long pants.

Don't poke around in snaky hideouts. Snakes like dark places like hollow logs and things piled up in the backyard. Don't stick your hands into these places.

Keep your eyes open. No one likes being stepped on, including snakes! If you are walking through long grass, stay alert.

Don't move. If you see a snake, stay as still as you can. Chances are the snake will forget you are there and move away. Even if the snake is coming towards you, or even slithers over your feet, try to stay still!

Don't try to touch or play with a snake. Snakes are dangerous and will bite if they feel unsafe. Don't ever try to play with a snake in any way.

Snakebite first-aid

If you are bitten by a snake, it is very important to act quickly and calmly. Here's what to do:

1 Keep still. Walking or running will move the venom through your blood more quickly.

2 Firmly wrap the bitten area with a bandage. Wrap your whole limb (so if you are bitten on your leg, wrap your leg). If you are bitten in a place that you can't bandage, just stay still and apply pressure to the bite.

4 If possible, apply a splint. This is a straight, solid object like a broom handle, a rolled up newspaper or a stick that will keep the limb straight and stop it from moving too much.

5 Call an ambulance or get someone else to go for help. Make sure you take note of the time of the bite.

SEA SNAKES

Fact File

▼

FOUND: Mainly in warm tropical waters around the world.

BREEDING: Gives birth to live young.

DIET: Fish, eels, fish eggs.

LENGTH: Between about 40cm and 3m.

TURTLE-HEADED SEA SNAKE
THIS SNAKE ONLY EATS FISH EGGS.

▼ Leaf-scaled sea snake

Small and quite rare, this snake has very small fangs and only a small amount of venom. It eats small fish and likes to spend time on the seabed, rather than close to the surface.

DUBOIS'S SEA SNAKE
THE MOST TOXIC OF ALL SEA-SNAKES.

FEROCIOUS FACT!

Snakes really do live everywhere, even in the ocean! Sea snakes look a bit like eels, with paddle-like tails to help them swim. Most of them live entirely in the water and can't move on land. Unlike fish, however, they have to come to the surface to breathe. Here are a few sea snakes found in Australian waters.

OLIVE SEA SNAKE
THIS GIANT
OF THE SEA IS
ALWAYS VERY
HUNGRY!

▼ Yellow-bellied sea snake

This sea-snake can swim backwards as well as forwards! It often comes together with lots of other yellow-bellied sea snakes to form floating rafts on the ocean's surface. They do this to attract small fish, which they then eat.

▼ Spectacled sea snake

This snake is quite long and slender, and very venomous. It can be found in the waters of northern Australia, where it eats eels.

▼ Horned sea snake

Spiny scales behind its eyes make this sea snake look a bit like a dragon! The spines probably help protect the snake's eyes when it puts its head inside narrow burrows.

◄ Stokes's sea snake

This is a venomous snake with big fangs and a big temper! It has a long, thick body and fangs that can bite through a wetsuit. A single bite can be fatal.

WANTED: SNAKES

Lots of people find snakes very useful, including doctors and their patients, scientists and farmers. These people want to use snakes for good reasons. Unfortunately, there are also people who want to use snakes for bad reasons, such as to sell overseas or to turn into products like handbags.

DID YOU KNOW?
Snakeskin is also used to make special types of musical string instruments in China and Japan.

SNAKES HELP US

Doctors and scientists use snake venom to help them make medicine for humans. To do this, they "milk" the snake by getting it to bite into a special cup to catch the venom. Snake venom is used to create antivenom which can save the life of someone who is bitten. Scientists are also using venom to develop medicine for serious sicknesses such as heart disease and cancer.

A SNAKE GIVING VENOM.

PEST CONTROLLERS

Farmers like snakes because they eat mice, rats, insects and other animals that can destroy their food crops. Snakes can be useful in the garden too, although you might prefer not to have a snake in your veggie patch!

SSSSTEALING

Why would anyone steal a snake? The answer is money. Many Australian snakes are smuggled out of the country and sold illegally for lots of money. If a person is caught smuggling a snake, he or she will be fined a lot of money and might be sent to jail.

YUM YUM

Some Aboriginal people in the Northern Territory hunt file snakes for food. They walk into muddy rivers and feel around with their feet and hands. When they find a file snake, they pull it out of the water and break its neck. Later, they cook the snake over a fire and eat it.

FEROCIOUS FACT!

Many people like to keep snakes as pets – they are easy to look after and only need to be fed every week or two. Some snakes can live in captivity for up to 40 years. You usually need a permit or a licence to keep a reptile as a pet.

GETTING TO KNOW SPIDERS

Spiders are everywhere! There are thousands of different types of spiders living all over the world – in hot, cold, rainy and dry places, on mountains and in caves, in trees and underground. Some spiders even live in water! Although there are many different types of spiders, they all have some things in common.

FEROCIOUS FACT!

Instead of having a skeleton on the inside as humans do, spiders have their skeleton on the outside. This is called an exoskeleton. It's similar to a hard, tough skin that protects the organs inside. When the spider grows, it has to shed this skin and grow a new one to fit. This is called moulting. The new skin is very soft at first, so the spider stays very still until the skin hardens and the spider is safe again.

▲ The athlete

Most spiders can't jump, but sometimes they move so fast that it seems as if they can. The jumping spider, however, can really jump! It uses special muscles in its back legs to help it leap forward. When jumping, it trails a web behind it as a safety net in case it falls.

▶ Enormous eyes

Check out the eyes on this net-casting spider! These huge eyes help the spider see in the dark – in fact, it can see better than a cat or an owl at night. Net-casting spiders have the biggest eyes of any spider in the world. They are also known as ogre-faced spiders.

DID YOU KNOW?

Most spider fangs aren't strong enough to pierce human skin.

FANGS

Fangs are scary but fascinating. A spider uses its fangs to pierce the skin of its prey and inject venom. This venom turns the prey's flesh into a liquid which the spider can then drink.

EYES

Most spiders have eight eyes, but some only have six. That's still a lot more than we have! The eyes are usually arranged in two rows at the front of the spider's head.

SILK SPINNERS

At the very end of the spider's body are the silk spinning organs called spinnerets. The silk is made inside the spider's body and then pulled out through the spinnerets by the spider.

QUEENSLAND WHISTLING TARANTULA

LEGS

All spiders have eight legs. At the end of each leg are special claws that help the spider move around on its web and grip onto different surfaces.

TRUE OR FALSE?

Some spiders spit on their prey to capture it.

A: True

PALPS

On either side of the spider's mouth are what look like short legs. These are called palps and they help the spider handle its food and explore its surroundings. Male spiders also use their palps during mating.

HAIR

A spider's body is covered with tiny, super-sensitive hairs. These hairs can do lots of important things, such as read the temperature and pick up on tiny vibrations. This tells the spider about its surroundings and helps it to hunt.

SPIN DOCTORS

A spider's web may look light and delicate, but don't be fooled – comparing strands of equal thickness, spider silk is stronger than steel. It's also incredibly useful. Spiders can use silk to capture and bind prey, protect their eggs, move around and, of course, make webs!

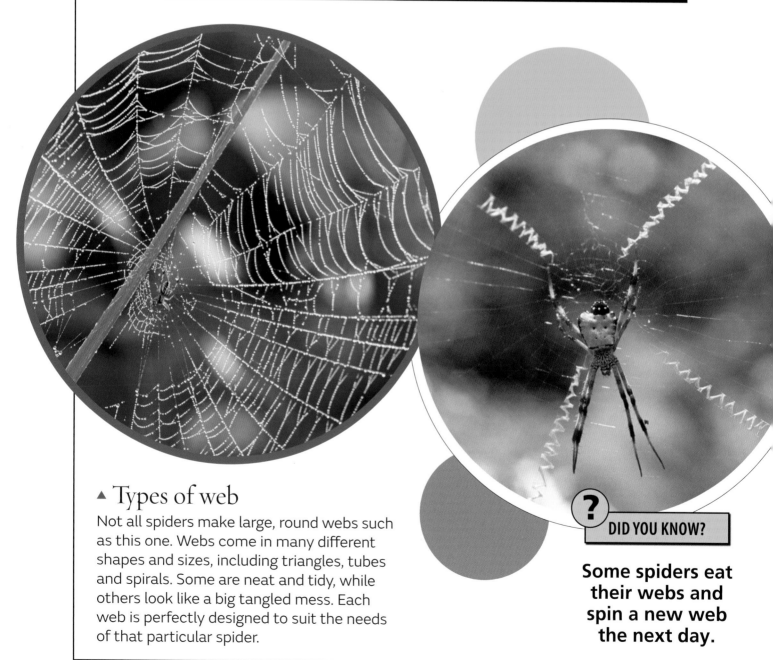

▲ Types of web

Not all spiders make large, round webs such as this one. Webs come in many different shapes and sizes, including triangles, tubes and spirals. Some are neat and tidy, while others look like a big tangled mess. Each web is perfectly designed to suit the needs of that particular spider.

? DID YOU KNOW?

Some spiders eat their webs and spin a new web the next day.

▶ Uses for silk

Spiders can actually make different types of silk, depending on what they need it for. For example, a web can have sticky bits for catching insects and non-sticky bits for the spider to walk on. If the spider needs to make a fast getaway, it drops on a single strong strand called a dragline. Some spiders also have special silk for wrapping up their prey (to eat later) or eggs (for protection).

◀ Super-strong silk

If you increased the size of a normal spider web so that the silk strands were about as thick as kitchen string, then that spider web would be strong enough to catch a jumbo jet plane. That's VERY strong!

FEROCIOUS FACT!

A spider has special glands inside its body that produce silk as a liquid. This liquid passes through organs at the end of the spider's body called spinnerets. As it comes out of the spinnerets, the liquid silk turns into a strong, stretchy fibre that the spider then uses to spin its web.

TRAPDOOR SPIDERS

Fact File ▼

BODY LENGTH: Up to 5cm. (about as long as a strawberry).

HABITAT: Australia-wide.

WEB: Up to 3.2m.

AGE: Up to 25 years.

HABITAT: Silk-lined burrow in the ground.

DIET: Insects that live on the ground, such as grasshoppers and beetles.

DEADLY FACTOR: 2/10

▶ Clever door

Not all trapdoor spiders have a door on their burrow, but this spider does. When the door is closed, it's impossible to spot from above because it is so well disguised with bits of leaves and twigs.

The burrow is a very useful place for the trapdoor spider. It is a safe place for it to hide from predators. It is also a trap for prey and a place for the female spider to lay her eggs and look after her spiderlings after they are born. The burrow is such a practical and cosy place that the female trapdoor spider stays there for her entire life – up to 20 years!

DID YOU KNOW?

The trapdoor spider has a spike on each of its fangs which help it to dig its burrow. It gathers the soil into a ball and kicks it out of the way using its back legs.

WEB DESIGNS

Some spiders have come up with very clever ways to use their webs. Here are a few weird and wonderful web designs.

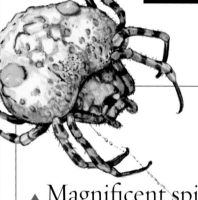

▲ Magnificent spider

This colourful spider is a bit similar to a fisherman. At night, it spins a single silky strand, similar to a fishing line. Instead of a hook, the line has a very sticky end. For bait, the spider releases a special chemical that attracts moths. When moths start to fly close, the spider swings the strand around until it catches one, then it reels it in.

▶ Redback spider web

The redback's web has two separate sections: a small, tube-shaped shelter, and a trap. The trap is made of a tangle of threads on the ground and some long, sticky strands leading up to the redback's shelter. When an animal bumps into the long strands, it falls into the tangle of threads and gets hopelessly stuck!

◀ Net-casting spider

This spider spins a net that is about the same size as a postage stamp. It holds the net in its feet and waits. When an insect passes underneath the net, the spider moves with lightning-fast reflexes, dropping the net and catching the insect. Then it hauls the net up and feasts on its prey.

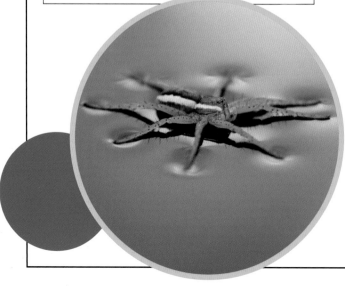

◀ Raft spider

The European raft spider doesn't have a web at all. Instead, it lives on the edges of swamps and rivers, tiptoeing across the water's surface using delicate hairs on the end of its legs. It mostly feeds on insects, but it can also dive into the water and eat animals such as tadpoles and even frogs.

▾ St Andrew's Cross spider

The St Andrew's Cross spider spins a big, round web with a bright cross running through it. Scientists are not really sure why it puts the cross there. It might be because the cross attracts insects, meaning more food for the spider. Or it might be so that larger animals, such as birds, don't accidentally fly into the web and break it.

CROSS-SHAPED WEB DECORATIONS GIVE THIS SPIDER ITS NAME.

DID YOU KNOW?

Some spiders spin a silken sheet to wrap their prey in after it has been caught in their web.

▸ Leaf-curling spider

To make its home, the leaf-curling spider pulls a dead leaf up from the ground on a silk thread. It then spins a tight web around the leaf so that it curls up to form a small hiding place for the spider. It's a good way to trick predators who think it is just a leaf caught in a web.

ON THE MENU

Spiders like to eat lots of different insects and some larger animals. But many different animals also like to eat spiders!

FEROCIOUS FACT!

Almost all spiders are carnivorous which means they eat other animals. Here are just a few of the things a hungry spider might eat:

- Bees
- Moths
- Ants
- Flies
- Mice
- Beetles
- Cockroaches
- Caterpillars
- Mosquitoes
- Larvae
- Frogs
- Lizards
- Other spiders

SPIDER SNACK?

This photo shows a spider wasp dragging a huntsman spider back to its nest. This wasp has a powerful sting that causes paralysis in its prey. Other animals that like to eat spiders include birds, snakes and lizards.

WOULD YOU EAT THIS SPIDER?

It looks pretty hairy and not very tasty! But in Cambodia, tarantulas like this are considered a special delicacy. They fry the spiders then eat them. Yum!

HUNTSMAN SPIDERS

Fact File

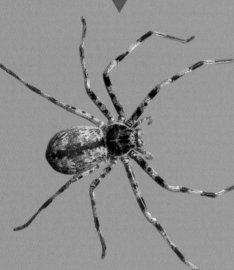

BODY LENGTH: Up to 4.5cm.

LEG SPAN: Up to 15cm (about as big as your hand).

HABITAT: Australia-wide; under loose bark on trees, under rocks or on plants.

WEB: None.

DIET: Mainly insects.

DEADLY FACTOR: 3/10

LIFE CYCLE

Different types of huntsman spiders make different types of egg sacs, but the female is always very protective of her eggs. The spiderlings are small and pale. They stay with their mother until they are big enough to leave and hunt for themselves. Huntsman spiders live for about two years.

FEROCIOUS FACT!

Huntsman spiders look pretty frightening with their big, long legs and hairy bodies. They also have a habit of scuttling out from behind the curtain in your house, or across the windscreen of your car, which can be a big shock! Although it looks scary, this spider is actually quite shy. In fact, it's probably more scared of you than you are of it.

SPIDER BITE!

Although they are small, many spiders can deliver a very nasty bite to humans if they are disturbed or threatened. Some spiders, such as the funnel-web, also deliver a killer dose of venom. Take a look at the illustration opposite to see exactly what happens when a funnel-web bites a human.

FEROCIOUS FACT!

No one has died from a spider bite in Australia in more than 30 years. This is due to the discovery of antivenom, a special medicine that stops the effect of the spider's venom. All major hospitals stock antivenom, so if you do happen to be bitten by a venomous spider, you will be okay as long as you get to a hospital quickly.

FIRST AID FOR FUNNEL-WEB BITES

1. Tell the victim to stay calm. If you can, call an ambulance. Remember that hospitals have antivenom, so the bite will not kill the victim.

2. Ask them to stay as still as possible. Moving helps the venom travel around the body more quickly.

3. Wrap a bandage tightly around the bite, then keep wrapping the bandage up the limb towards the heart. For example, if you're bitten on the finger, wrap the bandage up towards your shoulder.

4. If you can, attach a piece of wood or any other hard, straight object to the bandage to help keep the limb still and straight.

5. Call an ambulance if this has not yet been done.

FUNNEL-WEB BITES

▶ Spider in hiding

The funnel-web spider prefers to live in cool, dark, moist places. Spending most of their time on the ground, they can be very hard to spot! Funnel-web spiders live along the east coast of Australia, often in suburban backyards around areas with lots of rocks, shrubs, logs or bricks.

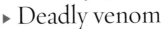

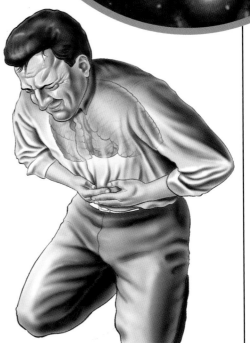

▶ Deadly venom

When the spider bites into the man's skin, it injects venom through tiny holes in its fangs. The venom travels quickly through the man's body. It contains many dangerous chemicals.

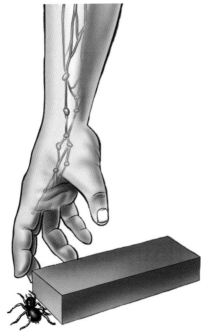

▲ Ouch!

This man would feel the funnel-web spider's bite straight away because of its piercing fangs and stinging venom. The pain is actually a good thing because it means the man knows he has been bitten and can seek help immediately.

▶ What happens next?

First, the man would feel pain and numbness in the area where the spider bit him. Not long after that, he would feel sick and start vomiting. As the venom spreads, he might start to experience bad muscle cramps and problems breathing. His heart would also have trouble beating properly. If he didn't get to a doctor, he would eventually die.

MOUSE SPIDERS

Fact File

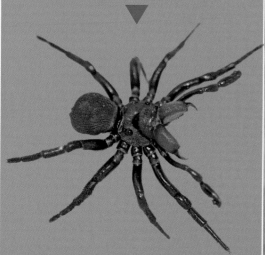

BODY LENGTH: 1–3.5cm.

LEG SPAN: 5cm.

HABITAT: Across mainland Australia, near rivers or waterways.

WEB: None – these spiders make burrows, usually with trapdoor entrances and just a few silk triplines.

DIET: Insects, small vertebrates, occasionally other spiders.

IN THE WIND

After red-headed mouse spiderlings hatch from their eggs, they will stay with the mother for a few months before leaving her. They spread out by 'ballooning'. They'll climb up to a high point and release thin silk threads that form a kind of parachute that allows them to float away. This can create a mesh of spiderwebs that covers the land.

DEADLY FACTOR:

7/10

TRUE OR FALSE?

Some mouse spiders have venom as deadly as the Sydney funnel-web.

A: True

Mouse spiders look very similar to other large black spiders, including the Sydney funnel-web spider. However, they can be identified by their short spinnerets, shiny carapace, big round head and eyes that are spread out across its head.

SEIZE THE DAY

Unlike other spiders, mouse spiders are often active during the daytime, while other species from the same family prefer to wander at night to avoid the heat and predators.

DID YOU KNOW?

There are eight species of mouse spider found across Australia.

KILLER SKILLS

These spiders use some pretty amazing methods to hunt their prey.

HIDING SPIDER

The lynx spider sits quietly on leaves or flowers, blending into the background. It has very good eyesight. When it spots a tasty-looking insect, it creeps out from its hiding place, sneaks up on the insect and pounces. It is a very agile hunter which means it can move and jump very quickly in any direction, similar to an acrobat.

COPYCAT SPIDER

The green tree ant-mimicking spider looks more like a green tree ant than a spider. Its disguise helps it in a couple of ways. First, it helps keep it safe from birds because they think it is an ant, and birds don't eat ants. Second, it means that the spider can walk straight into a green tree ant's nest and steal its larvae to eat. The spider fools the ants into thinking it is just one of them. What a trickster!

DID YOU KNOW?

Female spiders are the most commonly seen lynx spiders. Males are usually much smaller than females.

PATIENT SPIDER

The fringed jumping spider hunts other spiders, and it is a very clever hunter indeed. It taps on its victim's web to make the spider think it is an insect caught in the web or a male interested in mating. When the spider comes over to investigate, it gets a very nasty surprise! But that's not all. If one method of hunting doesn't work, the fringed jumping spider will try again. This is very rare in spiders! The fringed jumping spider is very patient and will keep trying until it finally gets its prey.

SNEAKY SPIDER

This trapdoor spider is sitting just inside its burrow. It is waiting for passing insects to come close. When one does, the spider will rush out and grab it.

SPITTING SPIDER

This spitting spider may look harmless, but it has a dark and deadly side. It silently sneaks up behind its prey, and when it's about a centimetre away, it shoots out streams of sticky, poisonous silk that instantly glues the victim to the spot. The spider finishes the job with a venomous bite, then wraps its dinner up in silk to eat later.

GOLDEN ORB WEAVING SPIDERS

DEADLY FACTOR:

3/10

Fact File

BODY LENGTH: 2–4.5cm (between the size of a $2 coin and a ping-pong ball).

HABITAT: Australia-wide, usually in dry forests or near the coast.

WEB: Large, in the shape of a circle.

DIET: Insects, small birds and bats.

BIG AND SMALL

The male golden orb weaving spider is much smaller than the female. Males often hang around the edge of a female's web, waiting for a chance to mate with her.

FEROCIOUS FACT!

The golden orb weaving spider spins a web that is a lovely golden yellow colour. Its web is huge, round and very sticky, and it is usually built in the spaces between the branches of trees or bushes, where it has the best chance of catching insects. Golden orb weaving spiders spin some of the biggest webs of any spider in Australia. Some webs are big enough to catch small birds or bats!

TRUE OR FALSE?

The orb weaving spider is one of the oldest types of spiders in the world. It has been around since dinosaurs walked the earth!

A: True

MASTERS OF DISGUISE

Lots of spiders can cleverly blend in with their surroundings, making them difficult to see. This is called camouflage. Camouflage is a very useful trick – it helps spiders to escape predators as well as surprise prey. Here are some spiders that use clever camouflage.

▼ Bird-dropping spider

Can you see a spider here? It looks like bird poo on a leaf, doesn't it? Look closely and you can see a spider hidden there. This is the bird-dropping spider. It spins a web that looks like a splash of poo. It then curls up in the middle of the web and releases a smell of dung, which flies find irresistible. When one comes in to investigate, the spider uncurls itself and snatches the fly in its powerful jaws.

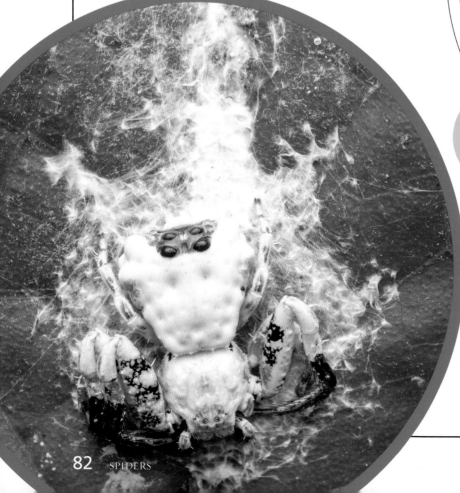

▲ Flower spiders

This flower spider is hard to spot against the bloom's white petals. It might look lovely and delicate, but it is a determined and ferocious predator. When a butterfly comes to feed on the flower's sweet pollen, the flower spider creeps up, reaches out its front legs and seizes the unsuspecting butterfly.

Wrap-around spider

This spider gets its name from its ability to flatten itself around a branch to avoid being noticed. This one even has a strange growth on its abdomen that makes it look like a twig. At night, it spins a web to catch insects, but during the day, it uses this disguise to help it 'disappear'.

▸ Long-spinneret bark spider

These spiders blend in perfectly with the trunks of trees, where they spin delicate, silky threads across the tree bark and around themselves. When insects walk across the threads, bark spiders quickly shoot out more web until the insects are hopelessly tangled up.

DID YOU KNOW?

Some spiders will 'play dead' to escape predators. They drop off their webs and lay on the ground with their legs curled up beneath them as if they are dead.

REDBACK SPIDER

DEADLY FACTOR:

10/10

Fact File

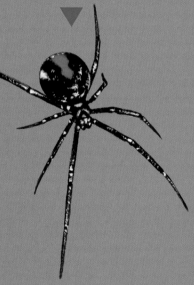

BODY LENGTH: Up to 1.2cm (no bigger than a thumbnail).

HABITAT: Australia-wide, prefers dry places.

WEB: Fine, cluttered, hung with dead leaves.

DIET: Large insects, snakes, lizards and mice.

DID YOU KNOW?

Only the female spiders have a dangerous bite. The tiny male spiders have fangs, but they cannot break through human skin.

The redback spider is one of Australia's most toxic spiders. If someone you know is bitten by a redback, do not put a bandage on as you would for a funnel-web spider bite. This will only make the bite worse. The best thing to do is apply ice and get them to a doctor or hospital as soon as possible. A doctor will be able to give them antivenom.

FEROCIOUS FACT!

Redback spiders love hanging around places where humans are. They are often found in backyards, garages, swimming pools and houses all around Australia. This, and the fact that they are very venomous, makes them one of Australia's most well-known spiders.

TRUE OR FALSE?

If there is a lot of food around, a redback spider can lay up to 1500 eggs in one season.

A: True

COLOURFUL SPIDERS

Many spiders have dull brown or grey colouring which makes them hard to see on the ground or up in trees. But some spiders are brightly coloured. They can use this colouring to blend in with leaves or flowers, or even attract a mate.

▶ Northern jewelled spider

This brightly coloured spider lives in warm tropical regions. Its body is very wide and it has very short legs. It also has six long, sharp spines on its body which makes it look even more unusual. It might look fierce, but it is very small and is quite harmless to people.

DID YOU KNOW?

The Christmas spider can change the colour of its abdomen very quickly. This makes it harder to see, so it's a good way of hiding from predators.

◀ Christmas spider

A close-up photograph of a Christmas spider shows the bright pattern on its 'body armour' and its six spines. These spiders often work together to build a large communal web that can be shared by hundreds of spiders. Passing insects fly into the net and get stuck, so there is no shortage of food for the spiders.

▸ Two-spined spider

It's easy to see how this spider got its name. Its two spines stand out from its small, round body. From behind, they sometimes look like eyes which is a good way to confuse predators. The spider hides under leaves during the day, but catches insects in its web at night.

MICRO SPIDER

This jumping spider is so small it could sit on the end of a pencil.

DID YOU KNOW?

Peacock spiders are also known as jumping spiders. They have very good eyesight and can jump on their prey to catch it.

▸ Peacock spider

The male peacock spider has bright, colourful markings on his body. He also has two colourful flaps attached to his body. The flaps are usually folded away, but the male raises them when he performs his mating dance, similar to a peacock.

FUNNEL–WEB SPIDERS

Fact File

BODY LENGTH: Between 1–5cm.

HABITAT: In damp, forested regions along the east coast from Tasmania to Queensland.

WEB: Many silk lines leading into their burrow or crevice.

DIET: Insects, small lizards and frogs.

DEADLY FACTOR:

8/10

DID YOU KNOW?
Males, with a 25mm-long body, are smaller than females, which grow about 10mm longer. But males have more potent venom.

TRUE OR FALSE?

The fangs of a funnel-web spider are hollow.

—

A: True

FAST FANGS

The Sydney funnel-web is the world's deadliest spider. If you have the misfortune of encountering one, it will put on a fierce attack display, lifting up its body, front legs and huge fangs as it prepares to lunge. Then it will thrust down frighteningly fast with fangs that are big enough to stab through a toenail. It has a highly toxic, fast-acting venom that killed at least 13 people between 1927 and 1980. Fortunately, no one has died since an antivenom became available in 1981.

Q & A

Q: How long is a funnel-web's fang?

A: About 6mm.

STINGERS, SNAPPERS & SLASHERS

Australia has its fair share of lethal animals that can sting, bite and cut.

STINGERS

Stingers differ from snakes and spiders because they don't use fangs to inject venom. Instead, they use various other things, like tentacles, to inject their venom into a victim while hunting or in self-defence. Depending on the animal, this venom can shock, paralyse and sometimes kill the target.

SNAPPERS

Australia has lots of potentially deadly biters. An encounter with one of these dangerous animals can leave you in severe pain for days, paralysed or even dead within seconds. A saltwater crocodile has the size and strength to rip you apart in seconds, while a bite from the much smaller Australian paralysis tick can leave you with a mild or even fatal reaction. The Tasmanian devil has the strongest bite of any mammal for its size – although you're unlikely to run into a devil as they can only be found in the wild in Tasmania.

AUSTRALIA IS HOME TO TWO SPECIES OF CROCODILE: THE FRESHWATER AND THE SALTWATER.

SLASHERS

Many Australian animals have sharp claws. This includes some of our beloved furry animals, such as wombats and kangaroos. Echidnas have sharp claws and a coat of sharp spines. But you're unlikely to be hurt by these animals. The most famous of our clawed creatures is the cassowary – read more about this giant bird on page 94.

▼ European wasp

European wasps are native to Europe, Northern Africa and parts of Asia. They have no predators (other than humans) in Australia. Unlike bees, European wasps can sting multiple times. They also release a pheromone when threatened that quickly attracts more wasps. So if you bother a nest, you may have to contend with the whole hive.

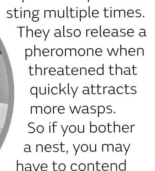

◄ Freshwater crocodile

Unlike the fierce saltwater croc, native freshwater crocodiles are generally not a danger to humans, with no recorded fatalities. However, this is not to say that they cannot be harmful if provoked. They are capable of inflicting serious injury in self-defence and will do so if threatened.

BLUESPOTTED FANTAIL RAY

▲ Stingray

Stingrays are armed with rarely used but dangerous probes at the end of their tail. When stepped on, threatened or if their vertebral column is touched, stingrays tend to thrust their spine towards the perceived attacker. This spine releases painful venom and causes deep lacerations that often lead to infection from bacteria.

◄ Native bees

Other than the species of stingless native bees, all other native bees have functional stings. With the smaller species, the tiny sting would be unlikely to penetrate the thickness of human skin, and pose little threat to us. Unlike the introduced European honey bee, these stings are not barbed, so the act of stinging is not fatal to the bee.

FEROCIOUS FACT!

While sharks, crocodiles and venomous snakes and spiders are a great threat to humans, bees and insects hurt humans most often.

Studies have found that bee stings, as well as other insect stings, account for more hospital admissions in Australia than spider bites and snake bites.

This is because a high amount of allergic reactions are caused by bee and insect stings, with many resulting in death from anaphylactic shock.

SALTWATER CROCODILE

Saltwater crocodiles haven't changed much since the time of the dinosaurs, more than 65 million years ago - and why would they? They are among nature's most effective killing machines.

TRUE OR FALSE?

Crocodiles give birth to live young.

A: False

FEROCIOUS FACT!

Each year, 1–2 people are killed by crocodiles in northern Australia, along with 4–10 non-fatal attacks. When they strike a large animal, such as a human, crocodiles usually grab the head or a limb and then roll in the water. This will either break the target's neck or drown it.

DEADLY FACTOR:

8/10

SAFETY TIPS

The best advice when it comes to crocs is to stay away from them! If you venture into saltwater crocodile territory, you won't stand a chance. These reptiles lurk stealthily, staying deadly still underwater for more than an hour at a time. When they strike, they move at lightning speed.

CROC SPOTS

Saltwater crocs are found in the freshwater river systems and coastlines of northern Australia. Mangrove swamps and riverbanks are their favourite attack zones, but they've even been spotted kilometres out to sea.

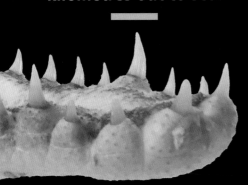

Fact File

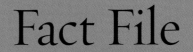

BODY LENGTH: Between 5–7m.

WEIGHT: Between 400–700kg.

DISTRIBUTION: Northern Australia from Broome, Western Australia to Rockhampton, Queensland.

HABITAT: Both tidal and freshwater areas including mangroves and rivers.

DIET: Reptiles, birds, cattle, buffalo.

DID YOU KNOW?

Crocodile babies are just 25cm long when they hatch. Males can grow to more than 6m and weigh a tonne. There are reports of crocs up to 8m long.

THERE'S NOT MUCH YOU CAN DO IF ONE OF THESE HUGE CREATURES WANTS TO MAKE A MEAL OF YOU!

SOUTHERN CASSOWARY

This odd-looking bird is a shy forest creature with a kick that can pack a deadly punch.

Fact File

HEIGHT: Up to 2m.

DIET: Mainly fruit, but occasionally also fungi, insects, fish and rodents.

DISTRIBUTION: Found in Australia only in Queensland in the Wet Tropics and Cape York.

HABITAT: Rainforests.

BREEDING: Females lay beween 3–5 large, greenish eggs a year. The male cassowary will then guard and warm the eggs. Once they hatch, the male cassowary will care for the chicks until they are up to 18 months old.

MOSTLY VEGETARIAN

Despite their fierce foot weaponry, cassowaries eat mainly fruit. In fact, many plants rely on their seeds being spread through the rainforest in cassowary poo.

DID YOU KNOW?

Cassowaries can reach speeds of 50km/h!

DEADLY FACTOR:

5/10

CASQUE CLOSE UP

These birds have a long neck and head covered in blue, scaly skin, as well as a pair of long, red skin flaps called wattles that hang from their throat. One of the cassowary's weirdest features is the large, grey, helmet-like lump, called a casque, that pokes out of its head by as much as 18cm. It's made of toughened skin – hard on the outside but spongy inside.

FEROCIOUS FACT!

Each foot has three toes and the the middle one is the biggest. It's up to 8cm long and, along with the other toes, is fitted with a dagger-like claw. These weapons are used to kick and slash at predators.

POISON VS VENOM

Venomous and poisonous don't mean the same thing.
They refer to the way that the animal uses its toxic chemicals.

If the toxin enters your body actively from a sting or bite, then that animal is venomous. Redback spiders, for example, use fangs to inject their victim with toxins. If you absorb the toxin passively by swallowing or touching, for example, then that animal is poisonous.

Some animals, like this Mozambique spitting cobra, are both venomous and poisonous. They can spit liquid that is absorbed through the skin as poison, and also inject venom with a bite.

Poisons are passive and are generally used for defence. Venoms, on the other hand, are active and can be used to hunt prey and fight off predators.

MARKS FROM A BOX
JELLYFISH STING.

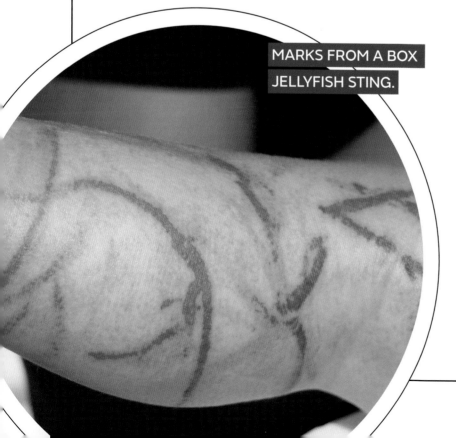

◄ Harm to humans

Venoms and poisons can cause pain and injury to humans, harm to our organs and even death. The danger does not just depend on the type of venom or poison, it also depends on what kind of animal it came from, how much was released into the person's system and where it entered the body. Rarely will animals try to hurt you, but if you do get bitten or touch something poisonous, toxins in the poison may impact your muscles, your blood or your nerves.

Platypus

The platypus is one of only a few mammal species that produce venom. Only male platypus are venomous. Used mostly during mating season, the barb of the male platypus is located above its back feet. Females are also born with the spurs, but they fall off before adulthood. Human stings have been recorded, and while not fatal, they have been known to cause severe pain and permanent handicaps around the affected areas.

THIS BARB IS ALSO KNOWN AS A SPUR.

▼ How we treat toxins

First aid and modern medicine gives you a good chance at survival if you're stung, bitten or cut by one of Australia's dangerous animals.

Antivenom is used to treat venomous bites and stings. It is produced by antibodies made by donor animals. Small doses of venom or venom components are injected into an animal such as a horse. The animal will naturally produce antibodies in response to the venom. The antibodies are then harvested through blood samples and the antibodies are separated out from everything else.

When injected into a patient, the antibodies that were produced by the donor animal gets rid of the venom.

◀ Hooded pitohui

This is one of the only known birds to be toxic. A songbird found in Papua New Guinea, the feathers of the hooded pitohui have one of the strongest toxins in the world, causing numbness and tingling in those who touch it. These toxins are a chemical defense against predators such as snakes, raptors and humans. The birds get the poison in their system by eating choresine beetles.

BOX JELLYFISH

Serious stings from a box jellyfish can cause death before paramedics even have a chance to administer an antivenom.

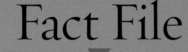

Fact File

DEADLY FACTOR:
10/10

OTHER NAMES: Sea wasps.

LENGTH: The bell reaches 30cm, tentacles up to 3m.

DIET: Prawns, worms and small fish.

DISTRIBUTION: Northern waters from Western Australia to Queensland.

HABITAT: Coastal waters, mangroves and estuaries.

BREEDING: Female jellies release eggs into the water which are fertilised by the males. That fertilised egg then attaches to rock or coral and grows into a polyp. Polyps can split into multiple jellyfish. It will eventually let go of the rock or coral when it has matured. A mature jellyfish is known as a medusa.

SERIAL KILLER

This is one of the deadliest creatures on the planet. Its fast-acting venom can kill an adult in less than five minutes. Each year it kills an estimated 100 people worldwide – more than crocodiles, sharks and stonefish combined. In Australia alone, box jellies have killed at least 64 people since the first recorded death in 1883. Their stinging cells work like high-pressured syringes, plunging into human skin and leaving life-long scars on survivors. You're most at risk of meeting a box jellyfish in coastal waters across northern Australia, between October and June.

BELLS AND WHISTLES

Box jellies have two main body parts: a bell and tentacles. The square-shaped bell grows as big as a basketball and weighs up to 6kg. Their tentacles each grow up to 3m long. The venom is stored along these 60 tentacles, in millions of microscopic stinging capsules called nematocysts.

FEROCIOUS FACT!

Box jellies will try to swim away from any large dark object, such as a human, that they detect moving about in the water. Unfortunately, they usually move too slowly to get out of our way.

STINGERS OF THE SEA

Jellyfish and bluebottles can't get out of your way, so if you know they're about, stay clear of the water.

DEADLY FACTOR: 9/10

THIS TINY JELLYFISH HAS CAUGHT A FISH.

◂ Irukandji

These species of jellyfish are tiny, with a bell about 2cm wide and tentacles up to 50cm long. But don't let its size deceive you! It causes one of nature's most painful experiences – irukandji syndrome. Each year, more than 60 people across northern Australia are hospitalised in agonising pain with this condition. Most people don't notice when they're stung, but about half an hour later, the victim develops severe backache, followed by a headache and agonising pain through their muscles.

FEROCIOUS FACT!

Australian doctor Jack Barnes deliberately stung himself, his son and a willing surf lifesaver with a jellyfish in 1964. He wanted to test whether it caused irukandji syndrome. It did! All three ended up in hospital. The jellyfish was named *Carukia barnesi*, after the doctor.

THERE IS NO ANTIDOTE FOR IRUKANDJI SYNDROME.

► Cone shells

Cone shells are marine snails that hunt other animals. They swallow their prey whole after catching and paralysing it using teeth that have evolved into large hollow spears. These teeth work like harpoons to inject venom. Some species of cone shells are particularly dangerous for humans. A serious sting can lead to pain, vomiting or paralysis. It may even cause a victim's lungs to stop working.

THIS CONE SHELL IS EATING A FISH.

DEADLY FACTOR:

7/10

DEADLY FACTOR:

6/10

DID YOU KNOW?

Even when bluebottles are dead, their stinging cells can still work. So never touch them, even when you see them lying on the beach.

◄ Bluebottle

Bluebottles are the most common cause of marine stings in Australia. Bluebottles aren't jellyfish – each one is a connected colony of different animals, relying on each other for survival. One part is the float, another part is for feeding and there's a part that reproduces. The bit to worry about is the tentacle. It can be almost 3m long and is covered in stinging cells. Although rare, deaths have been recorded. The intense burning sensation after a sting usually stops after an hour or two.

BLUE-RINGED OCTOPUSES

Normally these small marine creatures don't stand out. But when they're startled or threatened, they darken and start to pulse with glowing circles of shimmering blue.

Fact File

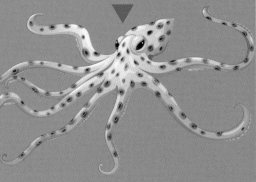

DEADLY FACTOR:

7/10

LENGTH: Between 7–10cm.

DIET: Fish and crustaceans.

DISTRIBUTION: Throughout the south-western Pacific, with some species specific to the Australian east coast.

HABITAT: Tide pools and shallow reefs.

BREEDING: Female blue-ringed octopuses only lay one clutch of eggs. They can lay up to 50 eggs in that clutch. The female guards the eggs until they hatch, not even leaving to feed. The female dies soon after the eggs hatch.

SMALL BUT DEADLY

These are the world's most lethal octopuses. These deadly creatures are usually perfectly camouflaged when hiding out in rock pools. But when they start to pulse, it's a clear warning sign to predators to stay away. Their bite barely leaves a mark and is usually so painless that it goes unnoticed. However, within as little as 10 minutes, the victim can feel a prickling, followed by numbness. Soon the victim will have difficulty breathing and swallowing, and is left fighting for their life.

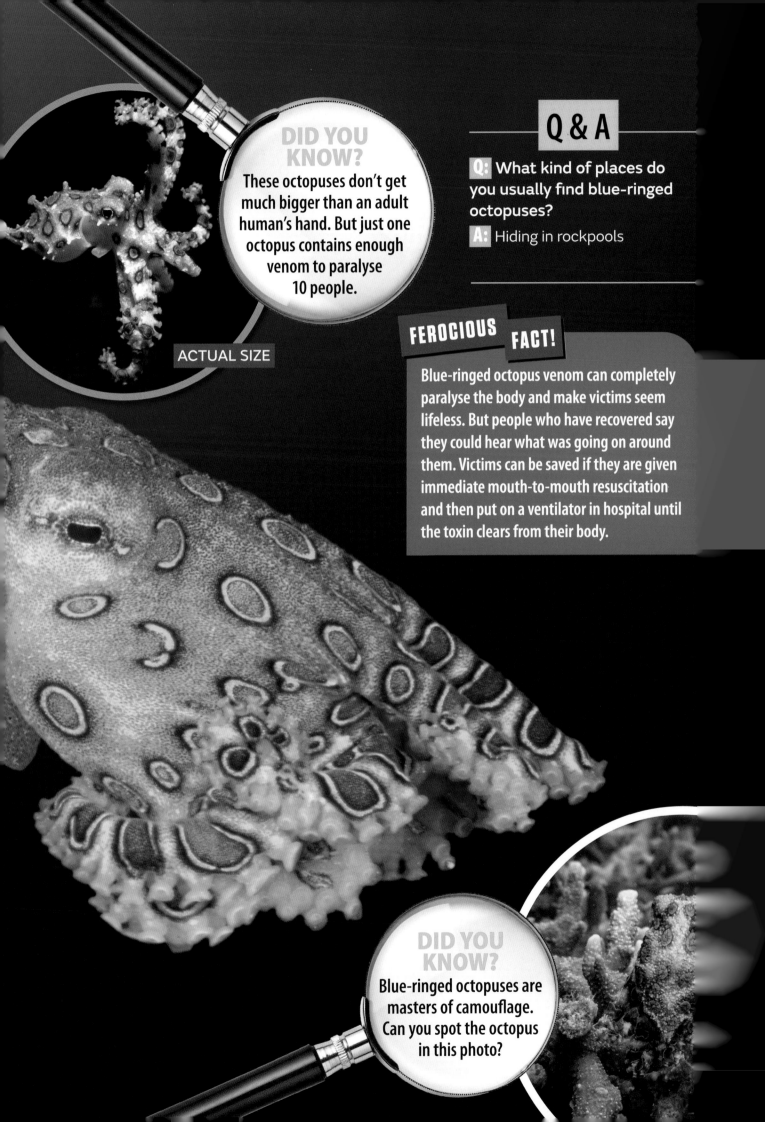

DID YOU KNOW?
These octopuses don't get much bigger than an adult human's hand. But just one octopus contains enough venom to paralyse 10 people.

ACTUAL SIZE

Q & A

Q: What kind of places do you usually find blue-ringed octopuses?

A: Hiding in rockpools

FEROCIOUS FACT!

Blue-ringed octopus venom can completely paralyse the body and make victims seem lifeless. But people who have recovered say they could hear what was going on around them. Victims can be saved if they are given immediate mouth-to-mouth resuscitation and then put on a ventilator in hospital until the toxin clears from their body.

DID YOU KNOW?
Blue-ringed octopuses are masters of camouflage. Can you spot the octopus in this photo?

Fatal Fish

Along with giant sharks, there are other deadly fish in our seas. These odd-looking fish mightn't seem as vicious, but they pack a serious punch!

DID YOU KNOW?

Lionfish are aggressive and territorial. They'll point their poisonous spines at a threat and swim towards it.

DEADLY FACTOR:

6/10

Common lionfish

The bright red on this species is a telltale warning sign that it's dangerous! It has 17 poisonous spines that it uses against predators and prey. Although lionfish have not yet been known to have caused deaths in Australia, people have been stung. It's said to be exceptionally painful. In the worst cases, the venom can cause hallucinations, paralysis and heart failure. Those most at risk are scuba divers and snorkellers.

Reef stonefish

This odd-looking fish has a sting so excruciating that the pain can cause muscle weakness, paralysis and shock - these factors may even lead to death! They have amazing camouflage that makes them blend in perfectly among reef rubble, so people often accidently step on one. It has 13 poisonous spines on its back. These are so tough that they can pierce shoes, as well as the feet inside. It raises these spines upwards when disturbed.

Smooth toadfish

Fry a fillet of the smooth toadfish and it's likely to be your last meal! Parts of the body of this pufferfish (its liver, ovaries, intestines and skin) are very poisonous when eaten, for both humans and animals! One study recorded 11 pufferfish poisoning cases in just over a year in New South Wales alone.

EUROPEAN HONEY BEE

This busy, buzzing little bee seems harmless, and it is for most of us. But for 700,000 Australians, it can be a deadly killer.

ALLERGY ALERT

Although ordinary honey bee venom, known as apitoxin, is poisonous to humans, it's not strong enough to harm most people. But it can cause a life-threatening allergic reaction in up to 3 per cent of the human population! This, combined with the fact that you can come across a honey bee almost anywhere, makes this creature potentially one of Australia's most deadly.

Fact File

LENGTH: Less than 2cm.

DIET: Nectar and pollen.

DISTRIBUTION: Throughout Australia.

BREEDING: The queen bee lays eggs which hatch into larvae, which are then fed honey by female worker bees. They'll mature into worker bees, drones (males) or queens themselves.

Q & A

Q: How long do bees live?

A: Up to five years.

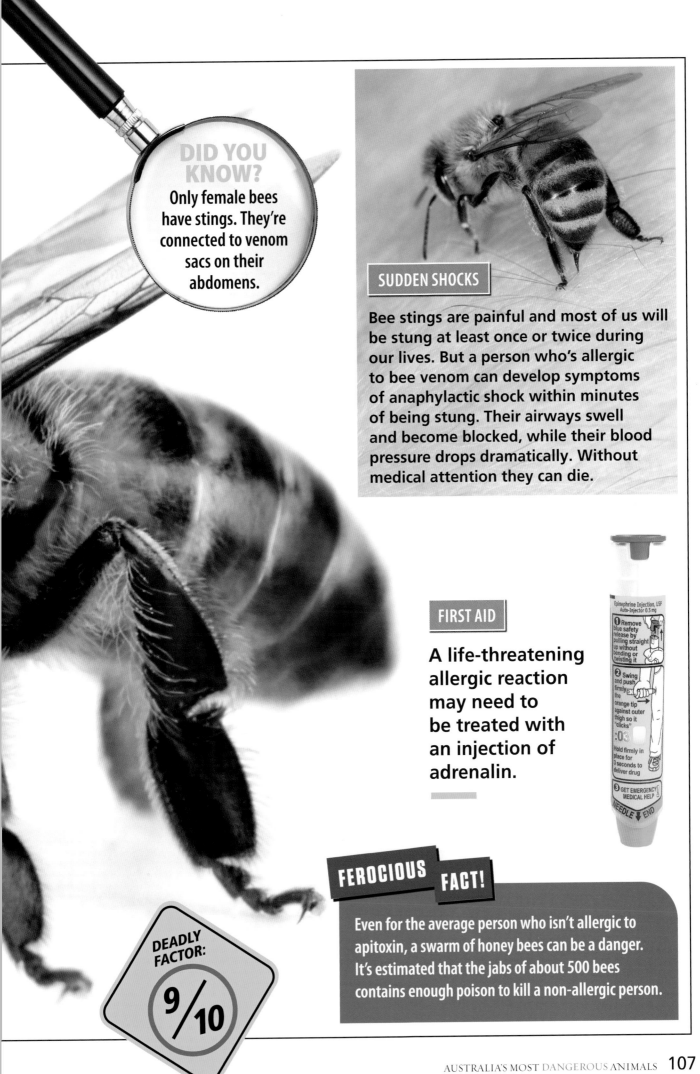

SUDDEN SHOCKS

Bee stings are painful and most of us will be stung at least once or twice during our lives. But a person who's allergic to bee venom can develop symptoms of anaphylactic shock within minutes of being stung. Their airways swell and become blocked, while their blood pressure drops dramatically. Without medical attention they can die.

FIRST AID

A life-threatening allergic reaction may need to be treated with an injection of adrenalin.

Epinephrine Injection, USP
Auto-Injector 0.3 mg

① Remove blue safety release by pulling straight up without bending or twisting it

② Swing and push firmly the orange tip against outer thigh so it "clicks"

:03

Hold firmly in place for 3 seconds to deliver drug

③ GET EMERGENCY MEDICAL HELP

NEEDLE END

FEROCIOUS FACT!

Even for the average person who isn't allergic to apitoxin, a swarm of honey bees can be a danger. It's estimated that the jabs of about 500 bees contains enough poison to kill a non-allergic person.

DEADLY FACTOR:

9/10

INFERNAL INSECTS

The first rule with these insects is to stay clear. If you are bitten or stung, it's important that you know your first aid.

DEADLY FACTOR:

5/10

Giant centipede

The bite of this multi-legged mini-beast can be intensely painful for several days. Thankfully, no one has yet been known to die from this creature's bite. They bite using a large pair of sideways-moving fangs that are really modified legs, known as forcipules. They contain poison glands that are found just behind the head. They grow up to 14cm long. Never poke them with a stick! Their many legs are each tipped with claws, making them exceptionally good climbers.

DID YOU KNOW?
Centipede mothers are devoted parents that guard their eggs and hatchlings by curling their bodies around them.

Australian paralysis tick

Most people only have a mild reaction to a paralysis tick bite. In some cases, however, it's so severe it can be fatal. When they bite us, they remain attached for a few days, feeding on our blood for protein. When they attach, they're just 3mm long. As they fill up on our blood, they swell to more than five times their normal size. After a few days, when they're full, they drop off.

DEADLY FACTOR:

5/10

DEADLY FACTOR:

5/10

Jack jumper ant

This carnivorous, scavenging insect is a large black and orange ant with a potentially fatal sting. Its venom isn't deadly to most people, although it makes the sting very painful. A very small number of people have an allergic reaction to it. In severe cases, victims can suffer an anaphylactic shock which can be fatal. On average, these ants kill someone once every four years.

SPECIES INDEX

* denotes a foreign species.

PHOTOGRAPHER AND ILLUSTRATOR CREDITS

Image locations are identified in order from the top left corner of the page.

3dsam79/Getty	28(1)
Theo Allofs/Getty	35(2); BC(1)
Andreas Altenburger/SS	32(1)
Greg Amptman/SS	17(2)
Sothy An/SS	71(3)
Attem/SS	108
Auscape/Getty	50(1); 51; 78(1); 81; 99(2)
Avalon/Photoshot/Alamy	47(2)
Fiona Ayerst/SS	10(3)
John Back/SS	24(1)
Beachy Photographs/SS	26(3)
Esther Beaton/AG	34(1); 38(1); 69(1); 70(4); 74(3); 75 (1-2); 79(2); 88(1); 89
Gary Bell	FC(6)
Kristian Bell/SS	39; 50(2); 52; 54(2)
Uwe Bergwitz/SS	53(2)
Bridget Bierschenk/SS	91(1)
Ullstein Bild/Getty	102(1)
Bildagentur Zoonar GmbH/SS	93(3)
Jonathan Bird/Getty	24(2)
BlueRingMedia/SS	102(1)
Chantelle Bosch/SS	83(2)
Br3ndy/SS	43(2)
Willyam Bradberry/SS	12(3)
BSIP SA/Alamy	41(1)
Andrew Burgess/Getty	71(2)
Andrew Burgess/SS	FC(5); 92
Robyn Butler/SS	68(3)
Anthony Calvert/AG	56(3)
John Cancalosi/Getty	34(2); 49(1)
Rich Carey	17(3); 99(1)
Roman Carretero/SS	9(2)
Katarina Christenson/SS	71(1); 73(1); 83(1)
Chip Clark/Wikimedia	7(4)
Rod Clement/AG	68(2)
Douglas Cliff/SS	24(3)
Clouds Hill Imaging/Getty	5(4)
Ian Connellan/AG	90(2)
Creatus/SS	60(1)
Marje Crosby-Fairall/AG	4(2); 6(1–3); 7(1,2,5); 11(2); 14(2); 18(2); 26(2); 30(2); 38(3); 50(3); 58; 68(1); 69(2); 72(3); 74/1; 88(2)
Curioso.Photography	BC(6)
Jao Cuyos/SS	103(2)
Ethan Daniels/SS	5(3); 26(1); 105(1)
Chuck Davis/Getty	8(1)
Kevin Deacon/AG	12(6)
Stephane Debove/SS	73(2); 80(2)
Alessandro De Maddalena/SS	10(1); 24(4)
DonyaHHI/SS	96(3)
EcoPrint/SS	90(1)
Levent Efe/AG	74(2); 75(3,4)
Eric Eichen/SS	85
Greg Elms/Getty	93(2)
Mart van den Elsen/SS	45(1)
Sherry Epley/Getty	37(2)
Dave Evans/Flickr	100(1)
Carol Farneti-Foster/Getty	36(1)
Fazwick/SS	95(2)
feathercollector/Getty	97(3)

The Fisherman/SS	98(2)
B.W. Folsom	9(1)
frantisekhojdysz/SS	5(1,2); 16(2)
Stephen Frink/Alamy	39
Stephen Frink/Getty	17(1); 101(2)
Don Fuchs/AG	48(1); 53(1); 57
Galexia/SS	56(1)
Getty Images	28(3)
Justin Gilligan/AG	7(3); 22(1)
Leonardo Gonzalez/SS	31/1
Mirko Graul/SS	107(1)
Ken Griffiths/Getty	41(2); 55(2)
Ken Griffiths/SS	37(3); 40(1–3); 43(4); 44(2); 45(2); 49(2); 55(1); 61(3); 66(1)
Ego Guiotto/AG	84(2); 91(3)
Gabriel Guzman/SS	43(3)
Roger Hall/Getty	94(2)
David Hancock/AFP/Getty	100(3)
David Hancock/AG	64(1,2)
Sean Heatley/SS	70(5)
Martin Helgemeir/SS	65(1)
Mark Higgins/SS	97(4)
Donald Hobern/Flickr	109(2)
Kurt Hohenbichler/SS	65(3)
Parmoht Hongtong/SS	83(3)
Anastasia Horova/SS	60(2)
Yann Hubert	16(3)
IHX/SS	49(4)
Eric Isselee/SS	49(3)
iStock/Getty	36(2)
Jackson Stock Photography/SS	33(3)
Apurv Jadhav/SS	65(2)
Alasdair James/Getty	68(4)
Jean and Fred/Flickr	66(2); 76(2); 77; 87(1)
Neg Kafou Photographs/SS	103(1)
Saurav Karki/Getty	87(3)
Patrick Kavanagh/Flickr	86(2)
Ken Keifer/Getty	13(1)
Amy Kerkemeyer/SS	107(2)
Mark William Kirkland/SS	33(4)
Kletr/SS	16(1)
Tomas Kotouc/SS	FC(4); 9(3); 10(2)
Johan Larson/SS	BC(4)
La-li/SS	82(1)
Lano Lan/SS	32(3)
Lindsey Lu/SS	23(1)
Paul Looyen/SS	FC(1,2); 62(2)
Cassandra Madsen/SS	87(2)
Somyot Mali-ngam/SS	79(1)
Matt9122/SS	11(1); 12(1); 18(1); 19(2)
Ted Mead/Getty	42(1)
Dudarev Mikhail/SS	23(2)
MPCZ/SS	4(3)
Nature Picture Library/Alamy	43(3); 100(2)
Nature Pixel/SS	87(4)
Nicolas Voisin/SS	20(1)
NOAA Photo Library/Wikimedia	20(3)
NoPainNoGain/SS	35(1)
Brittany North/SS	76(1)

Officina23/SS	12(4)
Paulo Oliveria/Alamy	20(2); 101(1)
Jurgen Otto/Wikimedia	87(5)
Martin Planek/SS	97(1)
Doug Perrine/Getty	11(3)
Peter Pinnock/Getty	14(1)
Stu Porter/SS	96(2)
Martin Pot/SS	63(2)
James Pozarik/AG	61(1)
Martin Prochazkacz/SS	4(1); 13(4); 28(2)
Torsten Pursche/SS	94(1)
Joe Quinn/SS	15(1)
Nick Rains/AG	55(3); 98(1)
Reptiles4all/SS	54(1)
Sylke Rohrlach/Wikimedia	105(2)
Zdenek Rosenthaler/SS	48(2)
Jeff Rotman/Getty	32(2); 33(1)
RugliG/SS	80(1)
Alexander Safonov/Getty	21(1)
Sail Far Dive Deep/SS	19(1)
Saulty72/ss	15(2)
Peter Schouten/AG	93(1)
Science Photo Library/Alamy	96(1)
Ian Scott/SS	12(7)
SergeUWPhoto/SS	13(2)
Steve Shattuck/Flickr	BC(2)
Sibons Photography/SS	42(4)
slowmotiongli/Getty	97(2)
Gerard Soury/Getty	28(4); 30(1)
Cameron Spencer/Getty	31(2)
Virginia Star/Getty	37(1)
Kevin Stead/AG	8(2); 22(2); 63(1); 95(1)
STR/Getty	61(2)
Oliver Strewe/Getty	33(2)
Aris Suwanmalee/SS	44(1)
Alan Thien/SS	82(2)
THPStock/SS	FC(3)
Richard Thwaites/AG	70(3)
Stephen Trainoff PH.D/Getty	25(2)
Tum3000/SS	25(3)
Tunatura/SS	91(2); BC(3)
Lee Yiu Tung/SS	47(1)
U278/Flickr	79(3)
VectorMine/SS	13(3)
VisionDive/SS	21(2)
Vkilikov/SS	12(5)
Wallenrock/SS	56(2)
Peter Waters/SS	106; 109(1)
Richard Whitcombe/SS	104
Wildestimages/Getty	2
Windzepher/Getty	25(1)
Tracey Winholt/SS	12(2)
Graham Winterflood/Flickr	86(1)
Pong Wira/SS	67; 72(2)
Mike Workman/SS	27
Peter Yeeles/SS	62(1); 70(1,2); 72(1); 78(2); 84(1); BC(5)
Tanto Yensen/SS	Ends

AUSTRALIA'S MOST DANGEROUS ANIMALS

First published in 2020
Australian Geographic
Level 7, 54 Park Street, Sydney NSW 2000
02 9136 7214
editorial@ausgeo.com.au
australiangeographic.com.au
© Australian Geographic
All rights reserved.

Author: Karen McGhee & Kathy Riley
Creative director: Mike Ellott
Art director: Harmony Southern
Designer: Melanie Coggio
Editor: Lauren Smith
Assistant editor: Peter Tuskan
Print production: Katrina O'Brien

Australian Geographic
Managing Director: Jo Runciman
Editor-in-Chief: Chrissie Goldrick

Funds from the sale of this book go to support the Australian Geographic Society, a not-for-profit organisation dedicated to sponsoring conservation and scientific projects, as well as adventures and expeditions.

Printed in Singapore by C.O.S. Printers Pte Ltd

A catalogue record for this book is available from the National Library of Australia

FSC
www.fsc.org
MIX
Paper from responsible sources
FSC® C016973